INK... and ME

Stories about Growing Up
on a Ranch in Texas

Marshall E. Kuykendall

THE 101

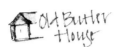 Dripping Springs

 Marshall

Old Butler House

 Barn

 101 Ranch House

'Machine Gun Nests'

Onion Creek

Hays City
X Corner

OLD   KYLE

← Wimberley

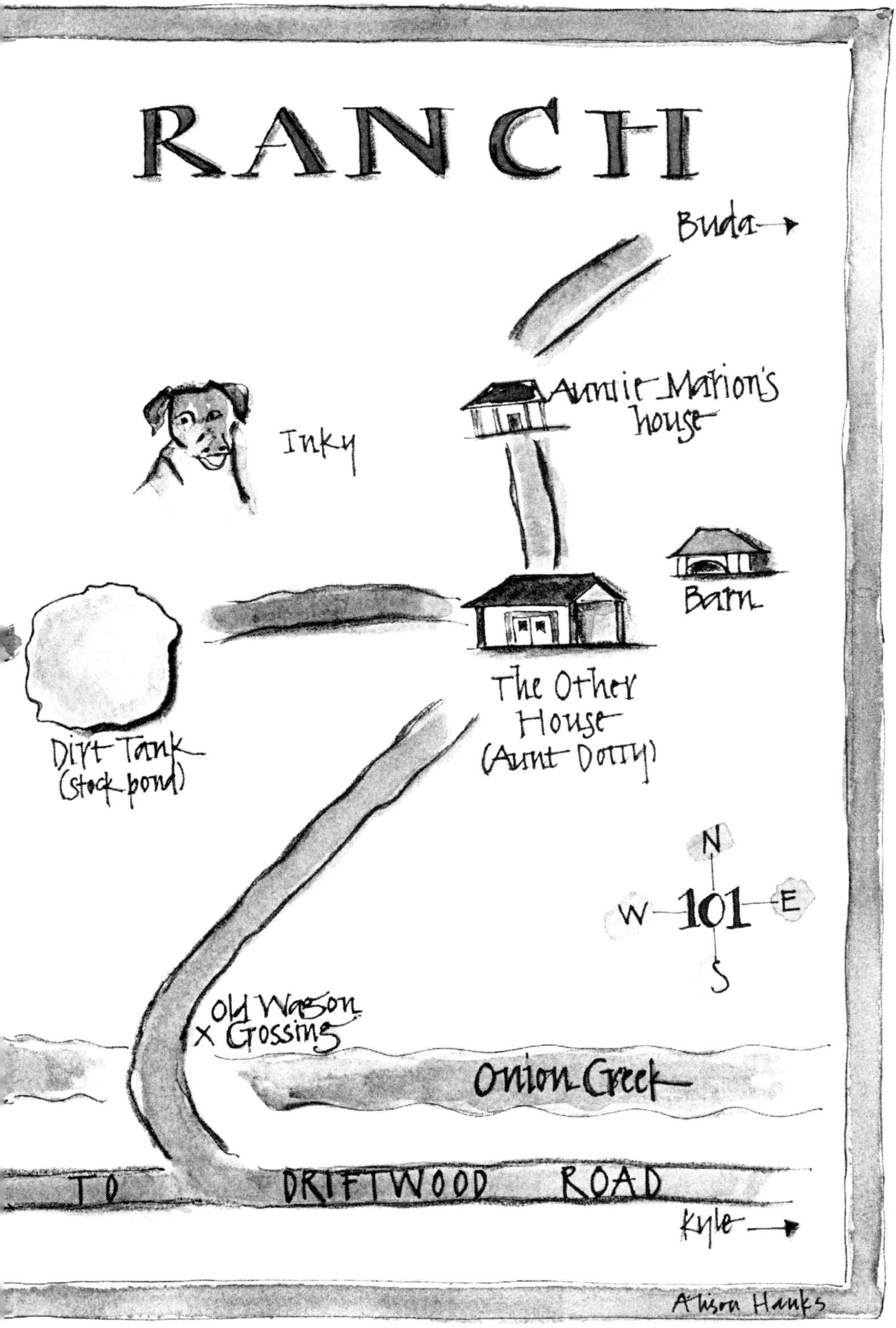

RANCH

Buda →

Inky

Auntie Marion's house

Barn

The Other House
(Aunt Dotty)

Dirt Tank
(Stock pond)

N
W — 101 — E
S

Old Wagon
X Crossing

Onion Creek

TO   DRIFTWOOD   ROAD

Kyle →

Alison Hanks

The map of the 101 Ranch is by Alison Hanks, who is considered one of the outstanding calligraphers in the country. She lives with her husband, Whit, in Austin, Texas.

All other artwork is the work of Jason C. Eckhardt. Jason is a freelance illustrator who has done work for Dell Magazines, Arkham House, and many other publications. He is the recipient of honors from the World Fantasy Awards and the New England Press Association, and enjoys illustrating children's books and other imaginative writing. He lives in New Bedford, Massachusetts, with his wife Jackie, a stepdaughter and five cats.

FIRST EDITION
Copyright © 2008
By Marshall E. Kuykendall
Published in the United States of America
By Eakin Press
A Division of Sunbelt Media, Inc.
P.O. Box 21235 ◫ Waco, Texas 76702
email: sales@eakinpress.com
▣ website: www.eakinpress.com ▣
ALL RIGHTS RESERVED.
1 2 3 4 5 6 7 8 9
ISBN 978-1-934645-58-1
Library of Congress Control Number 2008927710

This book is dedicated with love and affection
to our grandchildren:

Wylie

Jennie

Haley

and

Catherine

Contents

Author's Note ix
Background xi

Part I. On the Ranch with Mother and Daddy

When Speed Was Essential 3
Before Orville 8
The Rodeo 12

Part II: Early Days at Home

The Floods 19
Tie 'Em Hard and Fast 25
High Water 29
The Great Cleveland Parade 33
The Old Wolff Place 37
Varmints 40
The Tick 43
Central 47

Part III: Inky at His Best

On Safari 53
Helping with the War Effort 61
Fighting the Tanks 64
The Circus Was in Town 70
L. D. in the Corn Shucks 73
Aunt Dotty and the Sheep Killing 75

Part IV: SCHOOL, HORSES, AND HOGS

The Two Musketeers 81
Boys Will Be Boys. 84
The Ultimate in Fly Fishing 90
Horse Training 94
The Dude and the Wild Hog. 97
Never Unhorsed! 101
Sad Days 104

Part V: SMA, FOOTBALL

San Marcos Baptist Academy. 109
Six Man Football. 114
Six Man Football Revisited 119
Farewell, My Friend 123

Author's Note

I can distinctly remember the first book report I ever wrote in college about 100 years ago. It was on *Horses I Have Known* by Will James. When I got it back from Mrs. Hightower, it had so many red marks on the pages and in the margins that you couldn't even read the paper anymore, much less see the big red **F** that she had given me. And probably my three page long sentences would not pass Maxine Hairston's book writing class down at the big University of Texas either.

Seems the previous teacher I had somewhere back in my youth, who told me she loved my stories and to heck with punctuation and grammar, perhaps did me a disservice.

Some of these stories are about me and Inky, the black half-Lab, half-Shepherd who raised me. My folks sure didn't. Thank God, Inky gave me a good start.

Nevertheless, here goes some storytelling, written like I talk, not like I'm supposed to write.

—MARSHALL E. KUYKENDALL

Background

My family has been in Texas and living on ranches since they entered the territory in the early 1800s. Capt. Robert H. Kuykendall, my fourth great-grandfather, was a frontiersman who received a land grant from the Mexican government in 1824 as one of the earliest members of what is now known as Stephen F. Austin's Old 300. These were the first Anglo settlers allowed into Mexico/Texas in 1821 by the government of Mexico.

Austin's Colony, as it was called, settled mostly in southeast Texas, between the Brazos and Colorado rivers, all the way to the Texas coast. Robert would end up getting his leagues of ranch land from the Mexican government down in what is now known as Wharton County. When he died in 1830, he supposedly was buried in old Matagorda, which is presently located in Matagorda County.

So his son R. H. Kuykendall, Jr., and my great-grandfather Wiley Martin Kuykendall would ultimately be raised and have their ranches along the Texas coast in Matagorda County.

Wiley and his wife, Susan, who was the sister of A. H. "Shanghai" Pierce, had several children, but only three lived to be adults and of those three only Electra Miranda Kuykendall lived a normal life span. Both my grandfather, R. G. Gill Kuykendall, and his younger brother, Isaac, died very young. Grandfather Gill died at age 35 in 1905 and Isaac died at 20 in 1895.

My Grandfather Gill and his father, Wiley, sold out in Matagorda County in 1901 and bought ranches in Hays County which is just southwest of Austin and west of Buda and Kyle. Gill acquired 11,000 acres on Onion Creek (called the Hutchinson Place), where I was raised, and Wiley bought a 3,600 acre place on the Blanco River just two miles south of the other (called the Blocker Pasture). It was named after John Blocker, a famous Texas trail driver, who just happened to be a good friend of Wiley's, since Wiley was a pretty famous trail cattle driver himself.

Gill and Maggie Moore (my grandmother) Kuykendall had a bucketfull of kids but only four lived to be adults: my aunts Dorothy and Marion, my father, Wylie Moore Kuykendall, later called Bill, and my Uncle Ike.

When the 11,000 acres was divided among the four in 1933, my father got what was known as the Onion Creek portion and it was there that I was raised. Dorothy got the home place where the "Other House" was located. That was where Maggie, their mother, lived. That house which is known as the old Kuykendall place, was supposedly built around 1857 and Grandfather Gill made it much larger in 1902.

Dad was born in 1899 and even as a little boy was always into some sort of mischief. He had no father to guide him, so wild surroundings and a rambunctious nature led or pushed him through the rest of his life. I like to think he probably in-herited a bunch of it from his father. Gill was no saint. He was a hard-riding, gun-toting, whisky-drinking fellow, who nearly drove poor Maggie and her Aunt Eudora Moore, who lived with them, to an early death. As it turned out, though, it instead drove him to his early death.

The sisters, Marion and Dorothy, were several years older than Dad. Ike was the youngest. As mentioned, Dorothy lived in the old headquarters house with her mother. Marion mar-ried a prominent Cleveland, Ohio, doctor during WWI and didn't return to the ranch until about 1932, when she built her own house in the center of the 11,000 acres. She lived there as a recluse until she died in 1973. She had been a real beauty in her younger days.

Dorothy, the real rancher of the family, was great. When I visited her, she'd always have 13 lambs, four kids (goats) and three dogs in the main kitchen, feeding most of them from old brown beer bottles full of fresh cow's milk, that she herself milked that very morning. Grandmother Maggie and Dorothy were tough Texas ranch women. There was no work they couldn't do.

Bill, my dad, drove an open racing car all the way across the desert to California in 1918; he roped wild cattle in northern Mexico in 1925; he married Alice when she was age 15 in 1926; he sponsored a family ranch rodeo on the north end of their 101 ranch in 1929; he played polo all over the U.S. from 1930 to 1939; he bought a ranch in Mexico in 1956 and at the age of 57, bought and learned to fly an airplane with very few lessons and flew to his ranch in Mexico. He lived a rather flamboyant life to say the least, and dragged Alice along for the ride while he was at it.

Most people who knew my dad said he looked just like the movie actor Clark Gable. Grandfather Gill was a big man for the times, well over six feet. My side of the family got its height from the Pierces. Shanghai and his bunch, even the women, were big, tall people.

Mother, who we kids called by her given name, Alice, wasn't too bad looking either. She was 5'8" at 15 years of age, and made ol' Bill's heart jump plumb out of his chest the first time he saw her.

Some of the early stories that my father told me of his childhood happened after his father's death in 1905. Dad was raised loosely by his mother and also by the foreman they had at the time whose name was Joe Cruze. Dad went wherever Joe went. Some of the great stories, like roping the wild cow on the Shetland pony, came from that period.

Part I

ON THE RANCH WITH
MOTHER AND DADDY

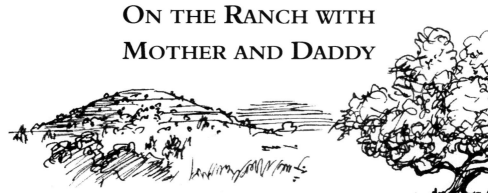

When Speed Was Essential

One of my fondest memories was of a mighty fine man who treated me like I was his own. When I knew him, Joe Cruze was an oldtimer from down toward Wimberley. He and his folks had been in the area forever. His father was a Civil War veteran, and Joe had been Grandfather Gil's foreman.

Joe always wore a Stetson hat, a red bandana around his neck, and a long sleeve shirt. Men of that period wouldn't be caught dead in a short sleeve shirt, wasn't manly or something. He would come driving in from his ranch down toward Wimberley and get out of his old truck and say "Howdy, have you heard any news?" He'd just been up to our house yesterday, but if you didn't answer, he'd holler louder, "I say, have you heard any news?" "No, Mr. Joe, nothing this morning." "OK, then let's get to work." He was a character!

After my parents and I moved to the south side of the ranch after World War II, Dad started using Joe to help build a bunch of high fence along our west line, so I got to visit with him a lot. He was always telling me stories of the old days.

Joe came to work for the folks right after they moved up here from Matagorda County. As I recall, the ranch was pretty much just one 11,000 acre pasture. If there were any cross fences in those early days, I don't remember him telling me. Later there were a bunch, so I'm sure that some existed earlier.

One of the stories Joe told me happened after Dad had learned to ride at four or five years of age and started following

Joe all over the ranch. Since Granddad died in 1905, when my Dad was only six years of age, I'm sure Dad latched onto Joe and went everywhere with him just like a puppy.

I have said many times in my life that the worst thing you can do for a kid is give them a durn Shetland Pony. If the animal's not biting you, kicking you, or running off with you, they just haven't had a good day.

Well, seems that Grandmother or Joe had gotten Dad a fine little grey-dappled Shetland pony with a flowing mane and tail. Dad thought it was the finest looking specimen in the whole territory.

The south end of the country was one pretty good sized cedar-break and working cattle down in that area around what we called the Hays City Corner was pretty rough. The cattle had plenty of screw worms in those days, 'cause that was long before they were eradicated. So once a week or so, Joe would work his way down toward that end of the ranch to check on the cattle that watered there and see if any needed doctoring.

Of course, Dad went with him, cowboy outfit and all. Seems that not only was Dad riding his fine new steed, but he was a-twirlin' his new thirty-foot cotton ropin' rope Joe had given him.

When they got down to Hays City Corner, there was a little bunch of mama cows down there that ran off a bit when Joe and Dad approached. They'd been watering in the dirt tank nearby, and as luck would have it, one of the cows had a case of worms in the top of her back. She'd probably crawled through the fence and got scratched and that's all it took in those days to get a good case of screw worms.

There was nothing to do but catch her and give her a good doctoring. Everyone carried medicine in their saddlebags for

4

this purpose and it was nothing in those days to rope an 800 or 1,000 pound cow or bull. You'd just give 'em a good dose of jerking down several times, then either tie 'em down or drag 'em alongside a good slim tree, snub 'em up tight, and doctor 'em all you wanted. Sounds easy, doesn't it?

Joe and Dad eased the bunch down into a corner where there was a little flat they could work in. Now-a-days it's all open country, but then it was as thick with brush and cedar as the hair on a dog's back. The plan was for Joe to crowd 'em up against the corner and when the cow broke back, he was going to put it to her. So Joe built himself a hefty loop and started into the bunch.

Dad could always rope anything that lived on this earth. Why, he'd been roping since he was probably two and could rope a rat with a string before it made its hole. Just natural talent, I guess. Anyway, unknown to Joe, while he was building his loop, Dad was building his. 'Course now, Texans tie their ropes tight to their saddlehorns and Dad had his plenty snug.

The cow was as big and rangy as the great outdoors and could probably outrun a racehorse. Joe knew he had only one chance to catch her before she hit the brush, when it'd be all over but the storytelling.

About the time the cow made her break, Joe applied about a pound of spurs to his big pony and with two big whips with the rope to the sides of his horse and one good chunk, he laid out a loop that would have caught the Empire State Building if needed, and as he later told me, "just missed her about this much," holding up his thumb and forefinger.

The All Mighty was with them on that day, and He prevailed to have the cow run pretty close to Dad. Dad spurred his little Shetland to action just as the cow went by him and laid a perfect loop right around her horns, head, and neck without missing a beat.

The cow must have stood sixteen hands, the story goes, and Dad's Shetland only three, and even though Dad was pouring the coals to his pony, the action really picked up when that rangy cow hit the end of the rope. The cow probably figured she had a gnat on a string.

The flat they were in probably covered about 300 to 400 yards at best and they luckily started down at one end. Looking at it from a side angle, here's probably what you saw: One cow running the fastest time a Derby's ever been clocked, followed by a little grey-dappled Shetland pony that was hitting the ground about every 45 yards, followed by Joe, who was really

whippin' his pony now, 'cause he had to outrun everybody before they hit the brush or you-know-what was going to hit the
fan.

Well, Joe barely made it and as luck would have it, his second loop was decidedly better than the first and the story came
to an end without having to peel Dad from some cedar brush.
I think Joe gave Dad one whale of a talkin' to, sold that Shetland
as soon as he could, but privately told everyone what a "fine
little roper the rascal was." *There are times when speed is essential!*

Before Orville

Our ranch was a haven for soldiers during WWI since Marion and Dorothy were of age in those years. Many an officer would travel all the way out from San Antonio to the Kuykendall 101 Ranch just to be with them. I am pretty sure Dr. Taylor was an officer at Ft. Sam Houston and that's how Aunt Marion met him. (They married later and lived in Cleveland, Ohio.) He invited her to some parties in San Antonio at the time. Some of the men were from Randolph Air Field because Dad told me some of them landed their "Jennies" (a WWI airplane) in the flats up above Grandmother's house and would take family members for a ride. Then as Dad became well known in San Antonio during the '30s during his Polo playing days, many officers from Randolph Field came out to hunt and fish with him.

I distinctly remember hearing planes one morning and ran outside the house just in time to see a Squadron of Stermans (an open cockpit trainer from the 1930s), all painted in Army Air Corp yellow with a big blue star on the side, come roaring right over our house, with the men in the open cockpits wearing helmets and goggles, waving as they went by.

People who believe that the Wrights were the first to fly early in this century have not learned all the facts. Just because theirs was recorded and the event depicted here was not, should not color the facts on who actually flew first in these United States.

One of the funniest stories I can ever remember Joe telling me was about Dad and the crane wings. Somebody found an old dead Sandhill Crane down by the stock tank and had cut off its wings and nailed them to the side of the barn. Dad was able to get them off and he tied them to his arms. He went around for several days running and flapping his arms. He said he "almost" came off the ground.

The old hay barn down at the "Other House" was huge. I barely remember it since it was torn down after the war. It had the normal horse and mule stalls underneath and up on the second story was a large hay loft that was as big as a gymnasium. The ceiling must have crested at fifteen to twenty feet above the floor.

Anyway, Dad hit upon the idea that what he needed was some height so he could *really* get airborne. He somehow found his way, not up in the loft, but up on the roof. The height of the whole barn was probably close to thirty or forty feet. He figured that if he got downwind on the very crest of the roof, and ran into the wind as hard as he could, he could take off by the time he hit the end of the roof-ridge.

For those of you who have never run down the crest of a steep tin roof, let me explain the procedure. You must run with one foot on one side of the crest and the other obviously on the other side. If you don't, the roof is so steep, you would just tumble off. Dad managed to crawl all the way up to the very crest and then he worked his way down to the leeward end of the barn. He was only about ten years old at the time and didn't weigh much and if his calculations were correct, he figured he would become airborne about midway down the ridge of the barn.

Dad got all ready and commenced to flap his wings as hard as he could and he told me they were working so good he "al-

most" came off the roof right then and there. With that he uttered the Comanche yell that he was to use so many times in his life and off he went running down the crest of that roof flapping as hard as his little engine could. The barn roof must have been fifty feet in length and he had a pretty good head of steam built up by the time he hit the end of the crest. Needless to say, he was not *quite* airborne yet, so he really put his heart into it as he went sailing off the end.

Folks in the country always raised a bunch of hogs in those days and that very fact was what saved Dad's bacon. Right off that end of the barn was a big hog pen that was full of slop and deep mud everywhere. He thought it was pretty funny that he didn't even get off one full flap after he left the end of the barn before he hit flat of his back in the hog pen. The splat of the fall almost blew the wings plumb off his arms and he lay there for a while trying to figure out whether he was dead or alive when it dawned on him he might get "hog et," so he up and crawled out of the mud-hole knowing that his flying days were over. (Actually they weren't.)

11

The Rodeo

Dad's brother Ike (Isaac) lived on the north side of the 11,000 acres and in 1933 when the ranch was divided, he carved out some 3,000 acres which would become his. There is a little white ranch house still standing there today and it was alongside the main road from Grandmother's house to Buda. I guess Ike must have built it, but I don't remember.

Ike was a big man and always very quiet, not like his older brother who was the consummate showman. Turns out he'd been a little on the wild side during his youth but as he got older, things seem to quiet down for him and that's the way I remember him.

Anyway, when there was a bunch of "doings" going on and cattle needed to be gathered, some family member would get on the old crank phone we had at the time and whistle at Ike to get himself down to the headquarters to help out.

One can imagine having to gather nearly 1,000 head of cattle weekly during the 1920s to eradicate the "Texas Fever Tick" that populated our area in those days. It was hard work. The ranch diary by Eudora Moore is filled with stories of hot, dusty men and bawling cattle during those tough days.

It seems that in the 1920s the high and mighty government decided to pass a law that required all states, especially Texas, to eradicate the dreaded fever tick. Laws were passed that all ranchers and ranches in Texas had to poison the ticks on all

12

their cattle. Since this was long before power sprayers and such, the only way to get rid of the little pests was to wash all the cattle in the state in some sort of poison.

The state and the government hit upon the idea to run all the livestock through a vat that was dug in the rancher's pasture. The cattle could be made to jump in this vat and swim out to the other side, thereby being immersed in the watery liquid that was full of poison, which at that time was mostly arsenic. The federal government not only required that this be done every twenty-one days, they also lent money or used federal funds to build "dipping vats" all over the state of Texas.

At the time, I think our family's 11,000 acre ranch was divided into about four pastures and I'm sure Grandmother and the family were running probably more than a thousand cattle on the whole outfit. So you can imagine the work it took, besides the torment that was heaped on the cow herd, to have to be gathered and dipped every twenty-one days, I think for a two year period to ensure the eradication of the little booger.

The family had introduced a good many Brahman cattle to the ranch and if you have worked a bunch of unruly cattle you know how tough it is to manage them. Throw in a bunch of Brahman cattle and it's a new experience.

Dad and Ike were among the cowboys one day, who were gathering a big bunch of Brahman cows, trying to push them into the corrals down at the headquarters ranch where the main ranch dipping vat was located. They would get most of the cows in the pen but every time the big bull went in, he'd get about halfway in the pen, then whirl and run over everything and everybody to get out again. The more they tried, the hotter he got, until all the bull wanted to do was fight. Nobody wants to tackle a big bull that's hot or mad on horseback, especially a big Brahman bull. What the bull will do is make a run at you, get under your horse's belly if he can, and with a pitch of his powerful head and horns, completely turn your horse upside down—with you on the bottom!

So Dad hit upon a plan. They'd let the cattle cool down for a bit and then they'd ease out around the bunch, get them ready, and make a dash for the pens. Once they had them and the bull inside, Dad would ride in with them and when Mr. Bull made his dash for the outside, Dad would lay a loop over his head and horns and break for the back of the pens to jerk the bull back that way. At the same time he wanted Ike to rope the bull from the back and they would stretch the old fellow out in the corrals between them.

Well, everything went like clockwork. They rounded up the bunch and made a break for the pens and got all the cattle in the corrals along with the big, bad bull, when Mr. Bull snorted and whirled to break out again. Dad had piled in with the bunch and when Mr. Bull broke for the outside, Dad laid a perfect loop over his head and broke for the back of the corrals. At the same time, Ike came busting in to catch him from the other way—but missed his loop. Dad said he was spurring the hell out of his horse to get as far in the corrals as he could when Mr. Bull, of course, going the opposite way, hit the end of Dad's thirty foot ropin'-rope that was, of course, tied mighty tight to his saddlehorn. When they both hit the end of that rope, it twanged like a pistol shot.

Mr. Bull was jerked completely around by the snap and Dad's saddle girt broke, and he made a double back flip, hitting the ground in a big cloud of dust about three inches in front of Mr. Bull's nose. *Still sitting in the saddle.*

Dad came out of that saddle in a flash, holding the saddle in front of himself, and fought that ol' bull all over the corral until he was finally was able to literally hang the saddle over the bull's horns so he couldn't see and then make a break for the side of the corral. He was able to scale the fence and get out of the pens before Mr. Bull could hook him in his sittin' down place. So much for working wild Brahman cattle.

14

Another funny story about Ike that Dad told me was one time when Mr. Joe and Uncle Ike hitched up the buggy for a trip into Kyle to get provisions. They hadn't gone very far down to the crossing on Onion Creek when they saw something fluttering and rolling around in the grass nearby. Both jumped out of the buggy to find an old owl had caught a big Prairie Racer snake and when he'd caught him, the snake had also wrapped himself around the owl. So a stalemate was in progress. Well, both Ike and Joe thought how much fun it would be to have a pet owl, so Joe got a tow-sack (feed sack) out of the back of the buggy and commenced to wrap Mr. Owl up in the tow-sack while they very carefully unwrapped ol' Mr. Snake. They unwrapped and uncoiled "everybody" until the snake was gone in the grass, or so they thought, and they had the owl in the tow-sack. Unbeknown to Uncle Ike was that as they had uncoiled the snake, he had crawled up Ike's pants leg and all was discovered when he tried to poke his way by Uncle Ike's belt. Dad said Uncle Ike commenced to holler and pitch and jump til he cleared about a half acre of brush. Ike lost his pants and the snake about the same time on the same jump. *All's well that ends well.*

Part II

EARLY DAYS AT HOME

The Floods

It seems to me that when folks get married and start living together that the inevitable is bound to happen that two little bratty
boys are going to show up whether anyone likes it or now. It just
goes with the territory. In today's time, Gil and I probably would
never have been born. Today, lots of couples who just don't want
to be bothered with kids just elect to not have them, since there
are all kinds of ways to prevent that sort of thing. In my Dad's
world that would have been perfect, and perhaps in Alice's, too.

My mother, Alice Hamlett, was born in Temple, Texas, in 1910
to a very prominent Baptist minister and his wife, William Alexander
and Faye Early Hamlett. Dr. Hamlett and Mona, as we called
Grandmother Faye, graduated together from Baylor University in
Waco, Texas, in 1896. Mona was the daughter of a well known
Baptist minister from Arkansas by the name of Marshall Daniel
Early. I am named after him. Mona was highly educated for a fe-
male of the 19th century.

Alice was the youngest of four children and only attended
high school. It was by happenstance that she was invited to a
dance in Lockhart, Texas, in 1925 where she met a dashing, wild
cowboy from Hays County by the name of Bill Kuykendall. One
thing led to another, and wild Bill talked her into marrying him
without her parents' consent and the rest is history.

My brother Gill was born in 1929 and I was born in 1932. I can
never remember a time that we didn't call her Alice. I suppose it
was because she wasn't much older than us, but I didn't start to
call her mother until very late in her life.

When Dad was gone a bunch in the 1930s playing polo all
over the country, we'd visit him sometimes in the summers. We

19

even lived in Shreveport, Louisiana, for a time when Dad had the ranch leased out to someone else. Other times, Alice would take us on trips around the area and one of her favorite places was Santa Fe, New Mexico. We'd go out there and spend several weeks in the Hotel DeVargas just off the square. It is now called the St. Francis Hotel.

Dad was a big hunter and he and his friends killed many deer each year for food. Alice got him to send off their hides to some company in Minnesota where they were tanned. Then Alice made them into the most beautiful gloves you ever saw and sold them to make spending money. Neiman Marcus in Dallas and Luchessee in San Antonio handled them for her.

It's funny what you remember about parents. I remember my father as being a giant of a man and always smelling of horse sweat. I was in awe of him. Alice was the disciplinarian of the two. Dad would just hit you but Alice would make us go break off a peach switch, lower our pants and switch the dickens out of us for some major offense, like running through the house with muddy bare feet.

She read stories to us every single night and our favorite was Uncle Remus. She also was very rigid about our manners and correct etiquette. We had to learn how to eat correctly, hold our utensils in the right way and know how to wait on the table in case we had guests. She was very strict about it.

I still remember the floods of 1935, 1936, or 1938. I said I could remember the floods, I didn't say I could remember which year it was. That was before all the dams had been built along the Colorado River so whenever we had big rains in the Hill Country, the Colorado would come roaring down and sweep through most of downtown Austin. My uncle Bill Hamlett, Alice's brother, was up from Houston during one of these periods and we drove into Austin to see the happenings.

Old Highway 81, the main north-south highway through this part of Texas, ran from San Antonio through Austin on its way to Fort Worth and Oklahoma and beyond. In those days, Highway 81 entered Austin from the south and as it got closer to downtown it became known as Congress Avenue. So you would enter about Slaughter Creek and head into the center part of town (that was all there was in those days) where the street would become South Congress Avenue and then slope down the hill past the Deaf School toward the old Nite Hawk Restaurant and the Congress Avenue bridge across the Colorado River.

Well, Uncle Bill and I got as far as the hill beside the Deaf School, when everything below us turned to water. The river was so wide below us that it came up the hill toward the school. It completely covered Riverside Drive, the Nite Hawk Restaurant, and all the houses and businesses that were located in that area. It must have been nearly a quarter of a mile wide below us. I'm sure it probably was over 1st Street but I don't remember.

Mr. Frank Spillar was a long time friend of the family and lived up in the Hills on a road that he put in called Spillar Lane. It is now in West Lake Hills.

He owned a bunch of rent houses down along Riverside Drive, so he rushed down to see what was going on with his  property. Just as he got close, one of his rent houses, which by then was completely surrounded by water, just popped up off its piers and started floating down the river, with all the inhabitants on top of the roof.

Mr. Frank rushed out into the water til it got about waist deep and hollered at the folks on the roof who he knew well. "Howdy Miz Mary, I see you got all the kids up there with you and you seem to be fine, but where is your husband, John?" To which Miz Mary replied. "Don't you wurry, Mr. Frank, weez all fine, and John, he done gone ahead on the privy."

I laugh every time I remember that tale Mr. Frank told me many years later. The house ran aground a short distance from its starting point and Miz Mary and all the folks, including John, made it to safety. When the bottoms dried up, Mr. Frank got a team of mules, some long beams and a set of old metal wheels and simply moved the house back where it was born, to wait patiently for the next big water.

Tie 'Em Hard and Fast

We had a big two-story ranch house where I was raised. Dad built it in 1918. It had the normal outbuildings—garage, wash house, warehouse, tools sheds and big horse corrals with some ten to fifteen horse stalls, tack room, and feed rooms—all scattered near and just west of the house. I remember spending much of my time with Inky trying to scout out some wild animal in the area or manning my forts during WWII in case we were attacked by the Japs or the Germans. I was a big reader. I had figured out that I wanted to be a Northwest Mounted Policeman and read all the books on *White Fang, Dog of the North* or *Spike of Swift River*. Dad thought I was crazy.

Buckaroos up in the high country of the western U.S. of A. do what we call dally ropin'. They swing about a forty to sixty-foot lariat or ropin'-rope. When they pitch their rope they keep a bunch of the rope coil in their off hand. As soon as they have caught the animal intended, they jerk down their throwing hand toward the saddle horn and as they do, they pick up some of the coil in the off hand and wrap in around the horn, in what is called a "dally." By taking up slack or letting off, they can control the animal they have caught and it's not so hard on man or beast.

Well, Texans like to do it the hard and rough way. Down

here we tie hard and fast to our saddle horn before we start and to make things more interesting, we only use about thirty feet of ropin' rope so the caught beast will hit the end sooner and that's more fun.

Like all little kids raised on a ranch what's the first thing you do that you can remember? Well, one, you learn to ride a horse, and two, you get yourself a little string or a cotton rope and you rope everything in sight. You rope the chickens, you rope the cats, you rope the dogs, you rope everything that will run close enough for you to get a whack at it—and drive everything and everyone absolutely crazy.

Well, you weren't gonna catch any flies on me. I was out and about with my windbreaker on, my Stetson pulled down tight with my little six-year-old legs just-a-pumping that tricycle as hard as I could go. My trusty cotton ropin'-rope was tied as tight as a big knot could get to the handlebars of my faithful steed. And I was easing up toward the hog pen where that ol' mama sow had all those baby shoats. I was a fixin' to rope me one.

The hog pens were built with an outside panel gate that could be raised so when the piglets got big enough, Dad would go and open that trap door so the mama could go and come as she wished. She'd come in once a day to be fed. Dad would open the trap door in the mornings and out she'd go. I figured if I would position myself by that hole, I could rope me one of those little suckers when they all came out the next morning.

The next morning I had all in readiness. When I saw Dad head out toward the pens I knew he was going to make his rounds. I peddled—I mean rode—out to be close to that particular corral. Sure enough, he fed the ol' mama last and went around and opened the trap door. I knew it would take her a bit to finish, then she'd be coming out.

I spurred my steed right up close and built myself a loop in readiness. About that time I heard, then saw them heading my way, so I kinda hunched up and got ready. But instead of coming out one at a time, they musta smelled me or heard me or something, 'cause just as they all got to the hole, there was a loud snort, and they exploded through that opening. You couldn't have gotten that ol' sow through there normally without a little bit of a squeeze, 'cause the hole was about as big as she was. Well, I'm here to tell you, I think they *all* came through there at once. There was one of the shoats that was a little reddish in color and I aimed to catch him if I could, but when they all busted out at once, I flung my rope in the general direction of the pile of piggies he was in. When the dust cleared, which was lightening quick, I realized I had caught the ol' mama sow by mistake.

My cotton rope was about fifteen feet long and tied mighty good to my handle-bars—I mean saddlehorn—and in two jumps and a snort ol' mama sow hit the end of it. You've seen pictures in later years of the Navy shooting airplanes off a carrier's deck using a catapult. They had nothing on me.

27

The only thing that saved me was I had turned in the right direction and was facing the way the bunch was going. There was a big grass flat out a ways from the pens for about 150 yards. We made that 150 yards or a good bit of it in about three or four big snorty jumps with me trying not to lose my balance and peddling as hard as a little boy can. I say peddling, but I think most of that distance I was probably airborne 'cause I was sure making some mighty good bounces. About the fifth or eleventeeth jump, my ol' steed and I parted company. As I rolled over in the air, through the cloud of dust I could see ol' mama sow just hittin' the timber below the flats with my little red tricycle doing the best it could.

About ten days later, Dad ran on to the ol' sow. She was still dragging my cotton rope behind her but to his surprise there was nothing left of my tricycle but the little red handlebars.

High Water

I guess since my faithful steed, the tricycle, had bit the dust, Dad decided I was maybe old enough to have the real thing.

When Dad wasn't ranching, he was playing polo. He always had a bunch of really fine horses and polo ponies on the ranch so one of my earliest memories is riding up on ol' Smooth with Dad holding me on. After that, when I was about three, Alice would get me on a little paint pony riding English. All real riders are supposed to learn English before you go to "stock," Alice always said. So for the first few years of my life I rode English.

My next remembrance about horses is Dad unloading a bunch of ponies after one of his long sojourns up east somewhere and he told me to come and take a look. About that time he got this big ol' gangly sorrel to back out of the trailer. I thought he'd never quit coming out. Man, he was big! Musta been close to 17 hands, with a big blaze down his forehead, and four white stocking feet. With that Dad turned to me and said, "He's yours if you think you can ride him." Being 6 or 7 years old with tons of experience riding, I allowed that I could!

His name was High Water and I suspect he was aptly named 'cause if he had ever gotten into any real high water, he'd a never known it 'cause he was so tall. Most folks think the first thing you got to give a little kid is a durn Shetland pony. Dad hated little horses and Shetlands in particular and I figured he was trying to get even with all the little horses in the whole world by giving me the biggest one he could find. I remember one of the pictures Alice took of me when I was riding on him, I looked like a gnat on the back of a long legged greyhound.

I was still riding English, not having yet converted, and I was all over the pasture having a great time. I think this might have been just before Inky appeared in my life, because it seems kinda separate somehow. Well, riding English on the tallest horse in the world has several interesting drawbacks. One, an English saddle has a funny little gadget right under the seat flap where you attach the stirrups. And if you push the stirrup way back with your foot it will unlatch and the stirrup will come off.

One day I was off down toward the polo field just north of the ranch house and for some reason I needed old High Water to "giddyup" just a bit faster than his plodding walk, so I commenced to kick him to go faster which didn't do any good, 'cause the harder I kicked the more he didn't pay any attention. I reasoned that was what Dad had told him to do, so I figured if I kicked him further and further back along his sides he might go better, but about that time the durn stirrup came unlatched and I hit the ground with a big thud and a cloud of dust before I could blink.

There I lay looking up and seeing plenty of stars, yet it sure was cloudy to boot. As my head cleared I found I was looking up at the underside of High Water's belly. He looked like he was three stories tall. There he stood as still as could be til I crawled out from under him. That's when it hit me that there was no way I was ever going to get back on him, him being 19 feet tall and all.

That's when problem number two came to mind. An English saddle has no piggin strings like a stock saddle has. On a stock saddle, you could jump up as high as you could and grab

one of the piggin strings and sometimes pull yourself up high enough where you could then grab hold of the horn and finally heave yourself into the saddle. Well, no such luck this day. There I was about a mile from the house and NO way I was going to be able to reboard, so I angrily flung the stirrup over my back, gathered up the reins and started down the road for the house. I remember that I hadn't gone any distance when some friend of the family came driving up, stopped and asked me if I needed any help, but I was still so mad over the happening that I blurted out "No, thank you," so with that they drove on and I continued on my way.

Later I figured out why Dad had given me this fine ol' polo pony. He was past his prime for polo but perfectly trained for a little boy. Dad might not know how to train little boys but he was one fine horseman. When you were on board, if you lifted one leg out of the stirrup, High Water stopped immediately. If you dropped a rein, High Water stopped. If you fell off, he stopped and would never move for fear he might step on you. And he would lean and push against another horse. All polo ponies are trained to lean into an opposing horse as they gallop down the field of play, to push the other horse out of the way of the polo ball so their rider can get a lick at it. So many's the time Dad and I would be riding, me on High Water and him on Smooth Sailing and I'd trot up alongside and we'd have a pushing match to see who'd win. Those were good times.

The Great Cleveland Parade

I own an old pair of worn chaps that are slick as a baby's behind from all the cat-claw brush that they went through years ago
down at the ranch in Mexico. I moved down there after leaving
the Air Force in 1957. We still had the ranch at Kyle, but after Dad
and Lat Maxcy (Gil's father-in-law from Florida) bought the
Mexican ranch in 1956, I stayed down there until the summer of
1960. Every time I have an opportunity to use my chaps now,
which is very seldom, I am reminded of Gardner (Gardy) Abbott
of Cleveland, Ohio and the 1939 Cleveland parade.

*B*y the end of the '30s, Dad was playing most of his polo
in Gates Mills, Ohio, a suburb of Cleveland. The Burton family owned the Hunt Club and the polo field there. They probably still do. One of their children is named Sarita, which I
thought was such a fine name that when I was blessed with my
second daughter, I named her Sarita, too.

Anyway, it seems that Dad somehow got involved with a
fellow from Oklahoma who had been playing either with or
against Mexican polo teams for some time. In the summer of
1937 he invited Dad to go with him to Mexico City to play
against the Mexican national team. I don't know who all four

players were, but Dad asked if he could invite Courtney Burton, a three-goal player at the time, to join them.

Courtney came down to the ranch at Buda and he and Dad went to the Mexican border where they were met with touring cars which escorted them all the way to Mexico City. After much "to do," they played against the Mexican national team and in the final analysis were beaten in the total tournament. As I recall, Dad said they had to play on borrowed horses that did not fare well.

The following year Dad invited General Jesus Jaime Quinones, the captain of the Mexican team to play against the United States team in Cleveland, Ohio. Alice and I had gone up there earlier that summer to be there for the festivities.

In 1938 we still had a large cavalry force operational in the army. Dad played against the army all the time. One of the Cleveland families Alice and I stayed with was an army captain's, and I think he was in the cavalry at the time. It was he who gave me my World War I lead soldiers that summer. He had a whole box of several hundred soldiers from that era, all dressed up in that period of dress and wearing the English style flat steel helmets. I found one man who was obviously an officer who carried a Thompson submachine gun, and from then on out that was me, of course! There was even a typist sitting at a table taking orders or writing orders for his commander. He was in a sitting position, there was his chair, the table and the little tiny typewriter. There was a group of fellows lying down with wire snips in their hands for cutting through barbed wire, and every kind of infantry man. They were fabulous, and probably worth a fortune today. Alice sold them without asking me sometime after the war, much to my regret. I would have never gotten rid of them. The only few I had ever lost were the ones Gil had melted in the skillet at the ranch when he was mad at me or trying to make a point of some kind.

So while Alice and I were rattling around from house to house, Dad had arranged for the Mexican team to be his and

Courtney Burton's guest in Cleveland and at Gates Mills. I don't remember where they stayed but I do remember the big party at the Hunt Club at Gates Mills 'cause one of the Mexican Army captains kept teasing me all the time and, of course, I remember the big parade. Seems that Courtney had arranged with the Mayor of Cleveland to arrange a parade for the Mexicans and give them a key to the city.

Now this was big stuff. I remember that the U.S. captain who had given me the lead soldiers was a friend of Courtney's. Dad and he were in charge of getting the U.S. Cavalry in the march. All I remember after that was the fact he had an open touring car, probably a Packard, which was the cat's meow in those days, and he invited Alice and me to ride with him in the parade. While I don't really remember a whole lot about that day, I distinctly remember sitting in that car and waving at the crowd.

This was probably in August of 1939. One month later, the whole world would change, because Hitler invaded Poland and in the invasion, wiped out the cream of the Polish Officer Corp, who just happened to charge the Nazi Panzer tanks with the finest of the fine—their cavalry divisions. They were wiped out nearly to a man, and the world's cavalry armies died that day, as did ours. The captain went immediately to war, changed from a horse to a tank, was desperately wounded by a German machine gun sometime in 1943 or 1944, and survived to live again in Cleveland. I saw him again in 1956. He and Gardy were members of some of the old families from there.

Also in 1956 when I was in Cleveland, I called upon Gardy and his family. He went upstairs to one of his closets and took out a box which he gave me to open. When Gardy had been down to the ranch earlier in the '30s, he had bought himself a fancy pair of Texas chaps to wear. When I opened the box, to my surprise, there was the pair of chaps, still quite new. They fit me perfectly and fared quite well with me when I was at the ranch in Mexico. As I said earlier, they are still very usable, but they have seen some pretty rough days. But you should have seen them when I took them out of that box that day!

The Old Wolff Place

When I was little and after Gil was gone from the ranch, Dad and Alice would take me to town whenever they had to go to a party or to the country club, or whatever. There was no one on the ranch to look after me, so I spent some of my early years ensconced in the best kitchens in old Austin or playing with the hired help at the country club. I'd end up going to sleep on a couch or something and when they got ready to leave, Dad'd come pick me up and haul me out to the old woody station wagon for the trip back to the ranch.

It was just one of those times that I remember so well 'cause I woke up about the time we hit the north end of the ranch with the car pitching and rolling, 'cause Dad was pretty drunk and hollering his head off about something. As I peeked over the top of the front seat I could see he was tearing down the old dirt road heading for the big corrals at the old Wolff Place. What Dad had seen in the headlights was the corral chock full of deer and he figured if he could get to the corral gate with his vehicle before all the deer busted out of that pen, he'd be in for one good ol' time. Time for what no one was sure, but we were fixing to find out.

As fate would have it, Dad slid the station wagon right into the opening with the front bumper against the far corner post and the left rear tire against the back one and with one big whoop and a holler, and "I'm gonna bulldog me that big ol' buck," Dad was out of that car in a flash, brand new tuxedo and all.

These were big old round corrals made out of long cedar rails with a horse trough in the middle. The deer had made the mistake of trying to get their nightly drink just as Dad had driven up. When the car approached, their first reaction was to bolt to the rear of the pens and that's what caught 'em. The headlights from the car blinded them and suddenly the gate hole was filled up with a '42 "Woody." Then a crazy animal in a tux tried to bulldog one of them and that's when the real fun began.

There must have been about twenty deer in the pen and several pretty good sized bucks, but one in particular had a hell of a rack on him. When Dad rushed in to grab one of them, they all broke in a circle round and round the corrals with Dad in hot pursuit. About the eleventeenth time that ol' big buck tore by, Dad nailed him. Well, "nailed him" is a misnomer. What Dad did was tackle him around the neck and horns and both went "head over tea kettle" in a hollering, bawling cloud of dust and torn tuxedo.

The strangest thing happened then. It got real quiet. I could see all these deer eyes over in one area just watching this big lump of horns and hair and tuxedo and dirt all piled out near the horse trough. Everybody and everything seemed to be waiting for the next comedy to begin. We couldn't tell whether ol' Mr. Buck had a hold of Dad or whether Dad had a hold on him. It seemed to be kind of a toss-up.

In the tense silence a little voice came floating out of the darkness over to where Alice and I were squinting, trying the see through the dust. "Alice, how in the hell am I going to turn this son of a gun loose?"

Varmints

In the early days of my life, I cannot remember a time when my father wasn't carrying his hunting rifle. It didn't matter whether he was horseback or in his truck, his ol' trusty .30-30 was always by his side. Times were tough in the depression years and there wasn't much to eat. For those of us fortunate enough to be born and raised on a Texas ranch, there was always wild game in the form of white-tailed deer, wild hogs, and wild turkeys. My father loved to hunt. I can still remember those venison backstraps, mashed potatoes and gravy.

As Dad got older he loved putting holes in four-legged varmints. Lots of them. His favorite hangout was down at Picnic. Picnic was his name for the lake down on Potter Creek where he could go and get away from Alice, to fish and shoot beer bottles he'd thrown out in the lake. I pity the folks that own that property now, 'cause if they knew the bottom of that pretty lake was strewn with about a million blown-up beer bottles, they'd probably never go swimming there again.

All that side of the ranch was deer proofed, which means the fence was 8 or 10 feet high, and Daddy hit upon an idea that gave him tremendous pleasure. He had been putting out cyanide guns for years to kill coyotes, and steel and live traps to catch coons and other such vermin, and he figured if he would hang all of them on the high fence for about a mile and a half for other varmints (any kind) to see, they wouldn't trespass on *his* ranch anymore.

The height of this adventure seemed to coincide perfectly with the advent of the lovely flower children who were sprouting up around the University of Texas in the '60s, who on fine weekends would saunter out in the fresh air of the beautiful Texas Hill Country in their rainbow painted Volkswagons and come around the bend of the road and run smack dab into Daddy's work of art. When approached from the downwind side, the effect was quite dramatic. The stench was so bad that it would make the hair slip on a grizzly bear, much less the scraggly hair of a mere hippie.

You could hear them howl in anguish all the way up to the house as soon as they realized that what they were seeing in this mile or so was about half of the coyotes, coons, possums, and skunks that lived in that part of the Hill Country. Daddy had been busy!

Of course, Daddy had seen them driving by, so as per usual, he had jumped in his old Ford Bronco with his twenty-four rifles and pistols on the seat beside him, and eased in behind them knowing full well what was going to happen just around the bend.

You see, this was part of his daily ritual. He watched every single car that drove by *his* ranch, down *his* highway, 'cause he believed that anyone who slowed down below 35 miles an hour had to be a potential trespasser and had to be watched, *or* followed. And he did just that, every day.

Just about the time all twelve flower children from the VW had made their third or fourth wail to the gods about you-know-what, old grizzled you-know-who drove right up behind them, got out of his tank with as many guns as he could carry, and demanded to know what the hell those damn hippies were looking at and how come they were stopping in front of *my* ranch, and stuff like that.

41

Well, those of you who like to hunt quail with a good dog know what "breaking from cover" means. You have never seen anything until you have seen twelve hippies trying to get in one small, foreign car at the same time. It was a sight that would warm the heart and it definitely warmed Daddy's. He thought those were good ol' days.

The Tick

Anybody knows when you live in the country you're gonna get full of ticks. It just goes with the territory.

I can always remember Alice making me take off my clothes to have a tick check every time I got in from the woods. The worst of those boogers were the seed ticks—those little devils that have just come out of their mother's shells. When they first hit on you, usually around the legs, it just looks like a blob of something so small you can barely see them. Well you'd better do something fast, 'cause that blob is going to expand right quick. When you next look at that spot it's gonna be the size of a dime, and then, sure 'nuff, it's the size of a silver dollar and growing. The best thing to do is pour kerosene on them right away, but if you are out in the boonies and near water, jump in and try to wash them off. If you're not near water, grab a bunch of grass and do your best to rub them off 'cause you are gonna have a heck of a time finding those little suckers when they spread out all over your little body and find all sorts of places to hide in.

During the depression, Alice and Dad took in "dudes." Now in my time, a dude was someone back east who came to Texas to visit a ranch, which obviously became know as a Dude Ranch. Well, we didn't have a dude ranch, but we did have dudes.

With Dad playing polo all over the country, folks naturally

started finding out that he lived on a big ranch in Texas and they all wanted to come have a look. Ours was the biggest ranch in the county and with all the fine fishing we had in Onion Creek, the prime deer and turkey hunting, not to mention an occasional bout with a wild hog, folks wanted to come and see for themselves.

Well, Dad had been playing polo one summer up near Cleveland, Ohio. While there in the late '30s, a fellow whose name escapes me, came down to spend the summer at the ranch. Dad and Alice charged $35 a person per week. That included everything. Alice told me that if only one person stayed they broke even, but if two came, they made a little money. Remember, the depression was still on so money was REAL money in those days. As I recall, he brought his daughter Sarita with him, and while here, they did all the things easterners like to do which included riding horseback, fishing, and other sundry outdoor activities.

To make the time here a bit more pleasurable, Dad and Alice offered to take the folks to Monterey, Mexico, which was quite an outing and of course they accepted. They were gone just about a week and upon their return I overheard Alice say she didn't think Mr. So and So was feeling real perky. Sure 'nuff, about two nights later while sitting at the supper table, Mr. So and So broke down and told everyone at the table that he thought he was dying of cancer. Well, everyone was shocked including me 'cause I'd heard of cancer but didn't really know what it was, so both Dad and Alice immediately asked how come he thought that and he said cause he had this big growth on his back and he knew it was a melanoma, whatever that was. Well, with that Dad jumped up from the table and allowed as how he needed to take a look 'cause he wanted to be helpful. They both retired to the other room so Dad could have a peek at what was troubling the poor dude fellow. After a second, we heard Dad's howl of laughter and about that time he came back into the dining room laughing so hard I thought he was going to faint.

It seems that when Dad pulled up Mr. Dude's shirt to have a look-see at this growth right slap dab in the middle of the dude's back, he came face to face with the biggest dog tick Dad said he'd ever seen. It must have been about the size of a full grown man's thumbnail, probably been there two weeks or more and was just about ready to drop off and hatch ten hundred million seed ticks. Well, Mr. Dude was so mortified he left the next day, and I started paying a whole lot more attention to my personal tick population after that.

Central

In those early days, riding horses from house to house and around the range wasn't the only means of communication. We had a crank telephone. It was a party line, a line that was shared by others. Our ring was one long and two shorts. It went, "rinnnnnnnng, ring, ring." And that was it. Any other combination belonged to other members of the family, either Aunt Dotty or Uncle Ike. Auntie Marion didn't have a phone.

The ringing was done by Mrs. Montague or "Central" as she was called before "operators" took over. She lived in a tiny stucco house on one of the main streets in Buda that led out of town toward Driftwood. I remember going into the "phone company office," as her house was called. It had maybe two or three rooms at best—the switchboard room, the kitchen, and maybe a small living room. I think her bed was in the room with the switchboard, 'cause she had to be close to the action late at night if a call came in. What made the house kinda neat was the fact that most of the ranch traffic that entered Buda came in from that direction, and Mrs. Montague could see who came and went. And that was important. That way she knew who was in town and who wasn't. She already knew the rest of the information, 'cause she personally had to direct all the calls. *She should write this book.* You see, anytime a call came in, a little gadget popped out of her big switchboard that let her know

47

where the call was coming from, then you'd ask her to ring so-and-so, and she'd do it. She knew everything that was going on in almost the whole world, or maybe at least Buda.

Now if we wanted to ring Grandmother, we just cranked in the rings that we wanted. But if we wanted to leave the ranch with any calls, we had to do one long ring and that got Mrs. Montague to answer. "Central" she'd holler, day or night.

It's hard to imagine these days that those folks like Mrs. Montague lived all over this country manning phones twenty-four hours a day for Ma Bell. I'm not sure that she ever had a single day off. I'm sure she must have but I just don't remember.

When you rang in, you never asked for a number, you always asked for Mr. So-and-So, or Mr. White's store, or please ring Sonny Cochran's house, or was Aubrey Lowden at home or had she seen Dad drive by. "No, Marshall, your Dad's not here. He's gone into Austin and won't be back til dark," and stuff like that.

Later on, we'd try to play tricks on her and ring in and then hang up like dumb little kids will do, and she'd ring right back, 'cause she knew who we were and where we were, and she'd say that if we didn't quit she'd have my Dad tan either both our hides or just mine in particular. That was enough to stop the funning.

I remember if you'd crank in a number then wait for the folks to answer, then stick the earpiece over the mouthpiece, it'd squall and blow them off the other end pretty good. I tried that on Grandmother one day and when Dad got home, I got my usual daily hollerin' and yellin' and whackin' that caused me to be rather sensitive where I sat for a day or two.

One time we'd been to town and right after we got home Mrs. Montague called to tell Dad someone had been in our house. We always told Mrs. Montague where we were going before we left, and during our absence, it seems someone had gotten lost and were obviously overjoyed at finding a house. They had probably "halloed" outside the house a bunch as folks would do in those days, and halloed themselves right into the house where they commenced to use the phone to find out where the heck they were. Mrs. Montague squalled at them and said that if Dad caught them in his house their hide would be hanging from the barn door come morning, and such as that. She lambasted him pretty good. He's probably still running somewhere.

It saddened us all when Ma Bell went mechanized and our "Central" was retired. We all complained for a time 'cause our source of information was lost forever and no one seemed to know what went on around the community. What's sadder still is now we just don't care. Just pick up the phone and dial a few numbers and someone in Paris answers and no "Central" has been involved at all. Sure miss Mrs. Montague.

Part III

INKY AT HIS BEST

On Safari

Inky just showed up in my life one day. I don't know whether Dad brought him home to us or whether ol' man Beverly Butler, who lived on Onion creek west of us, brought him to us. All I remember is one day Inky was in my life and things were a whole lot better because of it. In those days Dad didn't let the dogs in the house. I can still see Inky rolled up in a ball sound asleep out in the yard with it pouring down rain. Didn't seem to mind it at all, him being the outside dog that he was. If he had a so-called doghouse, I don't remember that either. He could have slept anywhere he wanted, in the wash house, or in the barn, but it seems to me he always liked it best out in the backyard, close to the live oak tree there and close to our back door, where he could meet me every time I went out in the yard.

I don't think we had dog food in those days like we have now. We fed Inky table scraps. Any and everything that came off of our table went into his dog bowl and he loved it.

I don't remember if we had any other dogs at the time, I don't think so. I can remember the deer fawns we raised each year but no puppies. Somewhere I have pictures of all of us in the back yard with the fawns and Inky, all together.

*I*t would seem to me that any great hunter could hear a big black stud horse approaching. But we didn't. How was I to know that ol' grey cat was going to run under him? And with me and Inky about three jumps behind him.

We were just getting the run into really high gear when ol'
Grey made the corner toward the hole in the oat bin. Inky
wasn't but a blink behind him and I was doing my all-out best
to keep up. How did I know that Daddy had come home early?
The calves he'd been looking for were right out in the middle
of the front pasture flats, all bunched up with the old mama
watch-cow, so all Daddy had to do was ease through them with
a quick count, make another little circle down by the tank and
within a little over an hour he was back at the tack room.

He had a bunch of horseshoes nailed up on the side of
the tack room where he'd hang his bridles. So when he
stepped off ol' Smooth Sailing, he just hooked the reins over
one of the horseshoes. The tack room was on the side of the
tunnel or ride-through. All the old barns in those days had
the ride-through. You know, the tack room on the left, the oat
bin on the right, with a roof across the whole thing to make an
area you could saddle your horse under and not get wet when
it rained.

Well, Daddy had obviously just stepped off ol' Smooth
when the grey cat run under him, followed by you-know-who
in rapid succession. Smooth, being well trained and well versed
in surprises, hadn't really reacted that much, but my father, not
being well trained and not liking surprises at all, came absolutely unglued. I thought he was old, but really Daddy was
only about 40 at the time, and many years on the polo field and
in the roping arena had not dulled his reaction time one iota.

Dad whirled to grab his rope from his saddle. He usually
kept it hanging loose over the horn instead of tied and this was
one day I was awfully sorry he had that habit. He grabbed me
by the scruff of the neck and commenced to give me three
really good whacks across my sittin'-down place. The rope
pretty well covered all it was intended for. When he finished
doing his best and hollering at me on what he was going to do
to me the next time he caught me chasing that cat, I figured I'd
been cured *forever*. Inky and I scurried off to hide in the hayloft

where it was safe and we stayed there until Alice called us in for supper.

Inky and I had spotted that durn ol' cat out near the tack room where Dad was saddling up. There was nothing we could do at that moment but look and plan our future attack. The two of us were deep in conversation about our future plans and just how we might manage to catch that ol' scoundrel when Daddy rode by. He reined up just as he passed as if a thought had flashed through his head. Turning ol' Smooth around, he moved up close to where Inky and I were having our little planning session and told us in no uncertain terms that if he caught us chasing that cat again today, he and I would make a personal visit to the wood shed. Being a very little boy and quite polite, I immediately jumped to my feet and stammered three or four times, "Yes Sir." "No Sir." "I won't do it, I promise," and stuff like that. And I meant it. Til I saw Inky cock his head to one side and I knew he'd seen something.

Sure enough Ol' Grey was easing around the tack room heading for the hay barn where the rats and mice hung out. Thoughts of *licks* and other such extreme *happenin's* went right out the window, before Dad was even out of sight. It didn't matter, though, 'cause I knew if he was just leaving now, it would be several hours before he got back. I overheard him telling Alice that he was going to make a "welta" down through the front pasture 'cause he was missing a calf or two.

That was enough for us two mighty hunters. We looked at one another as if to say, "Let's get on with it!" and off we went on our big safari. Now let me tell you, these things could not be attacked head on. It took some real military thinking, which Inky and I were good at. We knew Ol' Grey could not be caught without some pretty heavy maneuvering.

The corrals and pen were quite large. The tack room was

located in the pens where all the stalls were—must have been 20 or 30 of them—along with a big overhead oat bin where Daddy had the feed for the horses. He ran lots of horses 'cause of his polo days. The big hay barn laid about two pens back and both of us knew that if we got there first, we could lay in wait for Ol' Grey and give him a good run for his money. It wasn't a matter of catching him, it was a matter of *running* him! We didn't really want to catch him anyway 'cause a while back we'd come pretty close to doing just that and Inky still had a scab close to his left eye as a small reminder. The main thing was to get to the barn before he did, so we took off in a big round maneuver. By cutting through where the well house was we could take a shortcut and perhaps make it to the hayloft in time.

It took some doing but luck was with us and the timing was perfect. Inky and I were well hidden behind some bales when Inky saw him first. Ol' Grey was taking his sweet time coming. He knew the game as well as we did. I'm sure he'd heard Daddy give me that stern lecture and all, but his memory was shorter than ours was. It must have taken him 30 minutes to finally make it to the front of the barn. Most hay barns have open fronts for ventilation, so the hay will dry and not catch on fire after it's been stacked. (Sometimes folks will bale hay when it's a little too green and when it ferments it will get hot as all getout and burst into flames.) This hay barn was open in the front with the loft up above where you could throw the hay down into the milk cow stanchions and the mule stalls.

Anyway, ol' Grey was taking his fine time working his way into the front of the barn, looking and sniffing at everything he could think of. He was no fool. He must have been four or five years old, which as far as Inky and I were concerned was too durn old. It wasn't that we wanted to kill him or anything, it was just that we didn't care for any cats and him most particular.

Now you have to keep in mind that to really get the best of Ol' Grey, you had to run him at least one time around the

whole barn and halfway 'round the pens. Anybody can run something a few feet til they dive under the barn. What you had to do was cut him off from that particular escape 'cause then he'd take off for hole number two, which was under the oat bin and that would give us all a good run, which was what it was all about. You have never seen a more disgusted look on anyone's face til you have seen Inky's when the run wasn't good enough. I mean, why even get up in the morning if that was going to happen? He'd lay his ears kinda down on the side of his head and get that real funny look like I hadn't done my job right or maybe he hadn't liked my plan to start with. You have to remember, I was the General and he was just the Sergeant, and Sergeants have to do what they're told, even though they might not like it.

So the deal was to get up in the hayloft, but down on the lower end which would put Inky and me pretty much over the barn hole, so when we jumped him, he'd have to run the other way. There was a vertical ladder that we'd use to get to the top. Inky could climb them better than me, so he was always first up. He knew the plan anyway, 'cause (1) we'd talked about it, and (2) we'd only done it 4,000 times. Even ol' Grey knew it, maybe.

Well, Ol' Grey took a different route this time. Instead of coming up the slide where we slid the hay, he jumped up on one of the cross timbers and then jumped over into the loft. You can see Ol' Grey as he walked, stiff-legged, that kinda twitchy walk, all alert and all, like he was walking on egg shells and didn't want to make any noise, his tail stiff up in the air, snapping it on the end as he walked. He knew, we knew, and God the Father surely knew what was going to happen next.

Inky and I were so keyed up and ready to spring that we must of looked like an Indian's bow just before he shot his arrow. There's a funny thing about a hayloft. It's got a lot of loose hay on the floor of the loft, and that kinda loose hay was a lot like grease, or as Dad's favorite saying, it was slicker'n greased owl you-know-what. So there we were, the two mighty hunters, all crouched up and ready to pounce to start the great melee, Inky and me tremblin' like a hog trying to pass a peach seed. Inky would shake so bad that on occasions he would bolt before I had given the command and mess everything up. On those rare times, he'd come back all hunkered up and ashamed and telling me he was sorry, which I knew he was, and telling me that next time he'd be more patient which I knew he wouldn't, *'cause I couldn't either.* When Ol' Grey got to the magic spot—that was the spot where our bodies would no longer hold together—Inky and I sprung.

Well, sprung was *kinda* the way it was. What it really was, was ten legs running 80 miles an hour on loose hay for the first split second and not going anywhere. I swear, there would be hay flung eight feet in the air from the attempt to get started. 'Course, what always helps a cat are two things, first he's got claws, and second, Inky would bark. Not that he barked more than once. Usually he just barked to get things really going, and after that it was more of a running yelp or kinda howling as he ran. Well, I'm here to tell you, nothing gets a good cat race started better than that first *bark*. You can just see Ol' Grey doing that stiff twichy walk, knowing a mountain lion is going to get him at any second, instantly transformed into a ball of clawing cat hair trying to figure out which way to jump.

Once we'd all attained traction, Ol' Grey being first, it was hell bent for leather to see who could jump off the hayloft first, and in which direction. That was very important to Inky and me, 'cause if Ol' Grey made it off too quick, he'd double back and make it to the hole under the barn and the run would be over before it started, us with hamstrings and all. But if Inky could crowd him just a bit as they departed the loft, we were in business. Well, on this day they departed the loft like two turkey buzzards come sailing off the roost down on the Onion Creek bluffs. Ol' Grey, hairball and all, must have made twenty feet, with Inky, his ears in that flying position he always took when he was soaring at his best, right behind him, and me not being much of a flyer, trying to shinny down the ladder without getting too many splinters in my hands or legs as I slid down the wooden ladder.

By the time I had made it to the bottom, they had about thirty yards on me. It was then that Ol' Grey made a fatal mistake—he'd turned left instead of right. Turning right would have put him down the west side of the back of the horse stalls, which down the way was interrupted by a corn crib that was up on stilts. And all he'd had to do was dive under there before Inky could try to bite him in the butt, and the game would have been over. But providence was with us—he turned left. This took him down the north side of the stalls, which were in a **L** shape, all the way to the front, where another right-hand turn was necessary to get us all to the hole in the oat bin. Or I should say, get Ol' Grey there before we could beat him. Keep in mind that the big wooden gate down at the end of the back of the stalls where that set of pens ended, was slatted or spaced just like any big wooden gate is built. Those spaces are big enough for Ol' Grey to sail through but Inky had to dive under, and that split second saved him from a fate worse than death, or so Inky and I thought.

By the time Inky was able to dive and squirm under the gate, Ol' Grey had made the corner and turned for home. 'Course, catching a big tom cat by the butt has unexpected and absolutely assured results—that the other end will whirl around and claw and bite your face off. But in the heat of battle, one must be brave and to heck with the consequences.

It was just as I was clearing the gate that I heard Inky squall from around the corner and *I knew we had Ol' Grey at last.*

Helping with the War Effort

It was 1942 and the war was in full steam. Inky and I decided to do our bit to help out. On weekends, when I'd get home from the school on the days when there was still light after school, Inky and I fashioned three forts down in the pasture from which we could set up our machine gun nests. For some particular reason, they were all either east or north of the old ranch house where we lived. I don't think it was by any great design, it's just where Inky and I found three big live oak trees we could get up in to make our stand against the enemy. And maybe we built them there because it was near the road that came into the house and we could ambush unsuspecting travelers who happened to make the great mistake of coming that way when Inky and I were manning the armaments.

When I said live oak trees, I meant just that. Inky could climb a tree like a squirrel. He was a black part-Lab and and had the desire to always do what I did, so he followed me everywhere, always being my friend and companion until the day he died. Neither one of us would have had it any other way.

Anyway, for the next two years we must have killed 400,000 Japs. I remember the rare times that Alice took me into town to see movies at the old Queen Theater. It was usually on a Saturday, 'cause that was when the serials would run, and I could see the news and go back and tell Inky that we had been

doing well and we'd run to Fort # 1 and kill a few more enemies and protect the homestead.

A friend of Dad's fashioned our guns for us. He took a 2x4 and cut it off about two feet long. Then he bore a hole in the end where he glued a round dowel to form the barrel. Nails were placed along the top for sights, and one was hammered underneath for the trigger. Then he bore another hole at the rear end of the 2x4, the end nearest me, and inserted a short piece of the dowel at a 45 degree angle, and that became the pistol grip or handle for me to hold on to when I fired the machine gun. After that, we found some old black paint which really made them authentic. Then he put the whole thing on a tripod, and Inky and I were in business. As I recall we had two tripod guns and one free-holding BAR type, the reason being that two of the trees had areas we could sit down in and the other was more a tree that we crawled up and just hung on for dear life when the fighting got thick and heavy.

Inky was my scout and patrol officer. I would get up in the trees and order him out on a circuitous patrol, which he would undertake with great enthusiasm. Have you ever seen a coyote trot through high grass after a mouse? Well, that's the way Inky would go—halfway between a walk-trot and a trot-pounce. The grass being as high as it was, he'd have to kinda bounce up into the air so he could see which way he was going and also to see if any enemy was present. As soon as the enemy was spotted, which was usually on my shout, he'd bust and run for the tree and be up in it in a flash. He then always faced the rear, 'cause he knew I had my hands full mowing down the enemy in front and he didn't want us to be overrun from behind. In the heat of the battle, I'd shout "Are we all right?" and he'd always bark an affirmative.

Had the War Department known at the time how many Japs we had killed over that two or three-year period, I'm sure I would have received a medal and Inky would have been Army Dog Scout of the Year!

Fighting the Tanks

The sun rose that morning clear as a bell across the open plains and the waving grass was so wet from the dew that Inky and I could almost drink from their stems. Occasionally, I would see him lick some of the moisture off his hair to obtain a drink, a trick I had yet to learn, as bad as I wanted to.

There were times when Inky and I realized that there were just too many enemy tanks in the area and we had to do something about it. The front pasture laid to the south of our ranch house, and it was mostly open grass country with scattered live oak trees.

Interestingly enough, Alice never worried about Inky and me. I figure she knew we'd be all right. When I was very young, before Inky came, she had "belled" me. She put an old goat bell on me so she could open the front door and hear me tinkling as I played outside. Said I smelled like a goat for a year or two. Now that I was older and no longer had to bleat for my supper, Inky and I would tell Alice which way we were going, and with a warning to watch out for snakes, off we would go to find and destroy enemy tanks.

Inky spotted them first, the sun glistening off their armor. He rubbed up against me and pointed with his nose toward them. Sure enough, there were four, no five tanks, maybe a quarter of a mile slightly below us. You could see them glint and shine like a fresh silver dollar as the sun danced across their dew covered backs. They were moving at random, as if searching for us, kinda moving out in all directions. They probably knew we were on a search and destroy mission. Now all we had to do was move in closer and begin our attack.

These were not ordinary tanks, they were *super* tanks—armadillos! An armadillo is a funny creature. It always has four young ones that are of the same sex. It lives in one or more holes in the ground, which were usually located under a tree trunk or bush, and when boogered, it ran like the wind, making a real funny humming sound that Inky and I figured was its engine.

Now, our attack plan was totally different from attacking Ol' Grey, 'cause tanks weren't as sneaky and conniving as he was. We'd ease out into the open country, me with my trusty axe handle, and Inky with his favorite red bandana tied around his neck, so he could be told apart from the enemy. The reason I carried the axe handle was to battle the tank should one get too close to me and I had to fight for my life. Since a running small Lab can't do much of anything to stop a big fifteen pound armadillo. Inky's skirmishes involved trying to get his snout underneath the armadillo's shell while running at full speed and flip him over, which is no small feat. It rarely ever happened.

The deal was to keep the tank from reaching his hole, same as the cat. Once he reached his hole, you could never get him out. The game was over. An armadillo's hind legs are extremely powerful and equipped with long digging claws that will scratch the tar out of you. The other thing is, once he gets in his hole, even if you can grab him by his tail, you cannot extract him from his hole. His hind legs are much more powerful than one little boy, and any attempt to pull him out of his hole is futile, 'cause he digs those legs in the ground and that's it!

An armadillo's eyesight is very poor, but they could always hear or smell you if you were upwind from them. So, Inky and I started off across the pasture, on the alert to spot the enemy before he heard or smelled us. We'd scan way out in front of our positions just like hunting on the Serengeti Plains. Once we spotted one in the distance, we'd sit down right away and talk out our plan of action. My job was to find and guard the hole, hence the axe handle, and Inky's job was to wait til I had the hole covered and then take after the armadillo.

You could just feel the tension. Inky began to shake and I know it wasn't from the cold, being the middle of summer. Maybe it was 'cause we were both wet through to the skin from the dew, or maybe that's just what happens to you before a big battle. Anyway, we crouched up in the tall grass about 100 yards from the biggest one of the tanks, maybe one of those Tiger varieties. Anyway, we chose this one 'cause he was closest to us and we figured our nerves wouldn't hold out much longer if we didn't get on with the program at hand.

We had learned with much experience that when you first attacked one of these tanks, he'd break and run for his hideout, engine humming ninety miles an hour. If he made it, he could always attack us again in the future, so the game plan was to not let him make it to his sanctuary. No telling what havoc he could lay on us if that happened.

We eased our heads up above the wet grass to try and find where his hideout was. There was no brush, not even a tree anywhere nearby. Then Inky bumped me and pointed. Sure 'nuff, out in the very middle of the grass plain was an old cedar stump, and we could barely see some dirt pulled up along one side. That was it—his bunker. Why, if he made it to that bunker, he could draw down on us at will and let fly with those 88's and cause some real damage. No telling what would happen to Inky and me before we could get to cover.

Now came the tricky part. I had to work my way down and crawl up on the bunker and sit over the hole. I needed to perch there with my trusty anti-tank weapon, to pop him a good one when he came flying for his bunker. Maybe if I laid a good one on him I could divert him toward another bunker somewhere else and we could waylay him again before he could get to that one. Inky would attack on the side of the tank, trying to turn him over and I would be in hot pursuit trying to outrun them both to the next unknown hole in the ground. What a great skirmish!

Now while I was crawling down to get in position over the bunker, Inky was to make his way around to the other side of the tank and sit patiently until I waved or nodded my head. No word was ever spoken. When I nodded, the action was on.

Well, off we both went, Inky to do his job and me to do mine. He got in position a lot quicker than I did. He could crawl through wet grass a lot easier and quicker than I could, but nonetheless I finally made it. I eased up near the hole and kinda peeked inside. Boy it was big! One reason for the peek was, I might be just a kid, but both me and Inky knew what a rattlesnake looked and sounded like, and even though this was the heat of battle, it paid for me to glance down that hole before I placed my personal bo-hind on it. I could think of a lot of places to get bit, but on the bo-hind, *no thank you!*

I finally was ready and my heart was pounding away. Inky saw me get in place and he kinda raised up in his semi-racing position—sorta cocked like an arrow ready for flight. I remember seeing pictures of Babe Ruth in *Life* magazine, all bowed up at home plate, with his bat drawn up in his hitting stance, ready to knock it plumb out of the stadium. Well, you haven't seen anything til you've seen me, skinnier than a rail, all wound up over some gosh awful hole out in the middle of nowhere, holding a broken-off double-bitted axe handle that didn't weigh anything either and probably wouldn't hold off an attacking gnat, getting ready to hit a charging wild armored tank with claws at least three inches long right between the eyes. My heart was in my mouth.

It was either now or quit, and quit wasn't in my nor Inky's vocabulary, so I gulped and gave him the nod. The armadillo was probably a good fifty yards away with Inky about twenty

Eckhardt.

yards beyond him, but with my nod, Inky was on him like a panther!

Business picked up in a hurry. Here they came fast as a runaway locomotive coming down the track. And worse than anything, I was sitting on the station. You'd figure it'ud take 'em at least a bit to get to me. Well, I'm here to tell you, It didn't take three seconds. They were on me so quick that I barely had time to jerk back my trusty weapon and swing with all my might right at the tank's front end.

What happened then kinda seems funny now, but it was disastrous then. Not only did I miss him completely, but I laid my best blow right upside Inky's right ear, while the beast was tearing across my best pair of short pants that Alice had fixed for me, ripping a big hole in one side while he scratched a big gouge out of my skinny little leg with his durn long claws.

When the smoke and dust cleared, the armadillo was long gone and there we lay in the cloud of dust with not even a "Hi Ho Silver." Inky's head was all cocked to one side, as he tried to figure out what in the heck clobbered him, and I was scratched to all get-out, with my pants nigh about near gone.

What a pair we were with us both hobbling back toward the ranch house. Inky with his head kinda held to one side to help diminish the throbbing and me limping along trying not to let anything touch that big ol' scratch lest I die, hoping Alice would take pity on us both, and not put any of that dadgum ol' horse iodine on me that Dad always had available. Dad always figured what was good for a horse surely was good for little boys, but I'm here to tell you that horse iodine is worse than getting run over by a tank. Almost!

69

The Circus Was in Town

Haciano Rocha and his family worked for Dad for many years. I don't remember what his wife's name was, but I always called her "Madama." They had a bunch of kids and when things would get real dull, Inky would come and get me up at the big house where I was always reading about when I was going to become a Royal Mounted Policeman, something that bored him no end, and he'd remind me it was time to put on a circus. So I'd put *Silver Chief, Dog of the North* down til later, and off we'd go down to the Rocha's house to fetch them up for the circus.

After we'd told them what time to be up at the wash house, Inky and I would run around behind the washroom and get the two tall stepladders, stand them up, and while he stood on the bottom rung to steady them, I would drag up a long 2x4, which I laid across the top of both of them. We then borrowed one of Alice's dirty sheets from the laundry and hung it up in front to kinda create a stage effect. About that time, Madama and all her brood started arriving for the afternoon matinee.

The admission charge was a penny. Inky and I figured we ought to be paid something for our hard work—my brains and his work. As soon as we had everyone seated, which meant sitting on the ground, the wash pot, and the carpenter's horse, I motioned to the star to come forth. Inky would sashay out from behind the wash house in all his glory, his brand spanking clean red bandana tied neatly around his neck, and up to the top of the ladder he would go, just as slick as a button.

These old ladders were probably eight to ten feet tall, or so it seemed in those days. When you are only a little bitty kid, that ladder seemed thirty feet tall. But I didn't have to climb it, which was lucky 'cause I could start to climb up a wind-mill tower and when I passed the third rung my nose would bleed. *No Sir! Not Me!* Anyway it was Inky's job, and he loved it, sitting up there like a peafowl ready to take flight.

As soon as Inky'd hit the top, he'd squat and face down the 2x4 he was going to have to walk. I was down below with my new cape safety-pinned around my neck, Dad's cow-poking walking stick in my hand.

The deal was to make Inky do as many contortions on that little tiny board as one could imagine. I think it was about ten feet from ladder to ladder. So with all in perfect readiness, I snapped to attention, rapped the walking stick on the ladder a couple of times and pointed in the direction of the opposite ladder. With that Inky started gingerly down toward the other end, carefully putting each foot in front of the other on that flimsy board, balancing like a circus tight-rope walker. Sure' nuff, about the time he thought he was going to make it plumb to the other end, I'd shout "Stop." He'd freeze, then turn around. If you've never seen a full sized dog try to turn around on a little 2x4 bouncing up and down ten feet off the ground, you haven't seen anything. He'd start his front end around in sort of a doubled up **U**, with his hind end still facing the way he had started, and at the last moment, he'd just snap that hind end around just like it was a rubberband. Then I'd holler, "Sit"! and plop would go his butt, right smack down on that board.

The children loved it, since none had ever been to a real circus before, and Inky was delighted to oblige.

71

We combined everything we could think of, which probably took not over 10-15 minutes, that with the applause and all, at which time Inky would come down off the ladder, which was harder than going up. He would kinda look at me and say the show was over. Madama, who had only seen the circus about 400 times, would thank us in her best Spanish, pay the penny, and drag her bunch off to her casa.

L.D. in the Corn Shucks

*I*nky and I always enjoyed visiting with L.D. down the road aways. L. D. Bunton and my dad were about the same age, but while Dad was raised on the ranch, L. D. was raised just west of Buda in the Black Colony. His dad, Pete Bunton, was bronc breaker for my grandfather, and occasionally he'd bring L.D. to the ranch. No finer folks ever graced this earth than did Pete Bunton, his wife Mary, and their son L.D.

Dad had a big corn crib located in between some of the last horse stalls, and ever now and then when L.D. was working at the ranch, Dad'd have him get up in the corn crib and shuck a bunch of ear corn for the horses and the hogs.

On one particular day, Inky and I just happened to be saunterin' by in hopes of maybe gettin' a glimpse of Ol' Grey when L.D. halloed us from the crib. We crawled and jumped up into the crib, whereby L.D. showed me how to shuck corn. All that we finished we'd pitch out the door, forming a big pile out on the ground that L.D. was going to pick up later.

While we were working, L.D. would tell us tales of when he was a kid—stuff he and Dad got into when they were little together, all the while digging out more and more ears until he was kinda reaching down into a pretty good hole he had dug for himself. Well, I was struggling to shuck one big ol' tough ear when L.D. commenced to pitching and hollering and jumping til he was clean out of the bin and halfway across the horse pen.

Of course, Inky and I were frozen with fright and surprise,

73

not having the slightest understanding of what was going on. We figured L.D. had snapped his twig. When all the hollering and yelling stopped, we exited the bin with some haste and rushed over to where L.D. was standing, shaking like a leaf, to have him tell us that when he stuck his hand and arm down in the hole to fetch that last ear of corn, a chicken snake that had been hiding down in the pile of corn wrapped himself around L.D.'s arm. When L.D. brought out that last ear of corn, whom should he meet but Mr. Chicken Snake and *that's what caused the rodeo!*

After L.D. realized he wasn't dead, we all sat on the ground and laughed until our sides hurt. Inky wanted to go find Mr. Snake but figured it was best to let bygones be bygones. Corn shucks were still floating in the air.

Aunt Dotty and the Sheep Killing

*D*ad's two sisters and his brother lived on different parts of the ranch til Uncle Ike sold out in 1942. He sold his 3,000 acres to a road contractor named Greenhaw 'cause Ike said Dad came by all the time and told him what to do.

Aunt Dotty lived down at the "Other House," which is what we always called the big 1857 Texas-style house. It was about a mile and a half east of our ranch house.

Aunt Marion, who we all called "Auntie," lived over in the north central part of the ranch. She was a recluse of sorts. She'd been living pretty high on the hog for a number of years, married to some big doctor up in Cleveland since the war-to-end-all-wars. In fact, I think that's why Dad started playing polo up there. He'd gone up there about 1929 or 1930 to visit Auntie and started playing there after she got divorced. I don't think Auntie took the divorce too well, 'cause she holed up pretty good for years on her part of the ranch and, as I recall, didn't speak to Alice for twenty-five years til a horse hit her in the head and she was unconscious for thirty-two days. After that she thought better of it.

Aunt Dotty ran lots of sheep on her country. Dad had a sheep run under one of his horses one time. The horse was blind in one eye, and the crazy ol' sheep ran under the horse

75

on his blind side turning Dad "hind end over tea kettle" and breaking Dad's foot. He never ran sheep after that.

One day I heard a lot of commotion and loud talk out by the yard gate. When I looked out from an upstairs window, there was Aunt Dotty sitting on her horse hollering at Dad and pointing and waving toward Inky, who figured he'd better be in other parts 'cause he didn't like Aunt Dotty any more than she liked him. So he commenced to ease around to the other side of the house.

I hippity-hopped down stairs and out the back porch so I could get a little closer to the goings-on. It turns out that Aunt Dotty had lost a sheep or two the night before and she knew it was dogs that did it. She was demanding that Dad go check Inky's teeth 'cause Aunt Dotty knew he'd find sheep wool stuck in there. According to her, he was the only skanky dog in these parts that would do such a dastardly deed.

What was so strange about the whole affair was that Aunt Dotty didn't cotton much to Alice so she seldom if ever rode up to our place and when she did it was only to complain to Dad about something. The other thing that was funny was that Aunt Dotty must have had four or five old worthless dogs at her place and Auntie must have had twenty. But who got the blame? *My* one dog, Inky. I think she came over to raise Cain at Dad 'cause she knew it would upset Alice.

The thing about sheep-killing dogs is they most often run in packs or bunches, like a bunch of mischievous kids, egging each other on to bigger and better mischief. But Inky was a loner and very seldom left the ranch headquarters area. I'm not saying he was perfect, but killing sheep was just not his style, not that I'd've blamed him any, 'cause I hated sheep.

Anyway, Dad had me call him over and he checked his teeth and could find nothing stuck in them. So Aunt Dotty had to huff off toward her ranch without the crime being solved. Dad always figured it was probably Aunt Dotty's own no-account dogs that did the deed but she just wanted to come over our way and raise Cain 'cause there was nothing else to do that day.

76

Part IV

SCHOOL, HORSES, AND HOGS

The Two Musketeers

I was born in October so I didn't start school until I was nearly seven. Mrs. Miller taught first grade in Buda in the old building. I remember the classroom was down on the southwest side of the building. Miss Myrtle Watson was in the center room and Miss Katherine Bell was in the other end.

Mrs. Miller was a woman of some size who lived in a wonderful old two story home just east of the railroad tracks. My brother Gil took me with him to school every day and delivered me to her personally.

It was no time at all that I was running amuck through the halls, just as I did in the woods at home. Shortly thereafter, I flew around the corner of the hall and ran slap-dab into Mrs. Miller's ample midsection. She very neatly attached her hand to the scruff of my neck and took me into her classroom to give me the first and last paddling of my school career. I had been corralled.

Once I was forced to settle down, I discovered that it might be kinda fun to hang around with the other corralled kids. I remember there was Clyde Lowther, Aubrey Lowden, Dan Severn, and Sonny Cochran, this funny looking kid with the biggest ears you ever saw. There were others that I don't remember.

Well, Sonny and I hit it right off. One day, Dad cut some quarter-round for me and nailed a cross piece on the handle so

it would stay in my belt loop. We commenced wearing swords to school and it wasn't any time at all before we decided that we were the champion sword fighters of all times.

Sonny usually waited for me to get off the bus and we fought all over the school ground til Mrs. Miller came to get us and relieve us of our weapons. Then recess arrived and we were at it again. Sonny and I must have worn out a lumberyard of quarter-round that fall.

We were the two Musketeers and inseparable. We stayed friends for those early years, until I was sent away to another school, and I lost contact with him. Thirty years later, there was a knock on my door one day, and when I opened it, there stood this very big, older man with these funny looking ears. I took one look at him and hollered, "Sonny, is that you"? And he grinned and said, "Yes."

Boys Will Be Boys

I haven't said much about my brother Gil. It's probably because I don't have many memories of him and the few that I do have are somewhat unpleasant. He was three and a half years older than me, and by the time I can really remember, he was always gone. I guess that suited me just fine 'cause I didn't know any better.

When I started school at Buda in the first grade he was still around, and it was some time a little later that Dad and Alice sent him away. I use the term "sent away," 'cause that's what it was. I didn't know it til later, nor did I know what was in store for me 'cause I was too simple minded. Or little. No one figures that your mother and father care so little for you that they will farm you out to other families for years and years 'cause you are in the way, or because you are just "little" and a terrible inconvenience.

I don't really remember what year it was they sent Gil to live with my grandmother Mona—probably around 1940, just before the war. In later years I asked Alice why they sent me to live with folks around Buda, and she said it was 'cause I was sickly and she thought it was best for me. She never mentioned why they sent Gil away.

Before Gil went to live with Mona and then when he'd come out to visit the ranch, which seemed to be less and less as the years rolled by, he would always involve me in all his athletic activities as well as other more nonsanctioned activities.

One day Gil either found or dug up an old butcher knife. In order to see what kind of an edge the blade had on it (Gil had a very curious interest in the unknown.), he decided to draw it across my lower left leg to test its ability to cut. It was very effective.

Another time, we were playing hide and seek and after the game we were all thirsty. Gil said he'd go get us a Coke. He did, kinda. He found an old Coke bottle which he peed in and brought it to me to drink. Of course I drank part of it 'cause, as I said earlier, I was simple minded.

Another time we were playing war with real BB guns, and things were getting kinda hot and heavy with all the running and shooting at one another. Gil slipped around the corner of the house and when I stuck my head around the corner to see where he was, he shot me between the eyes.

Or the time Gil got me to tell a joke at Mrs. Hacker's dinner table where we ate lunch everyday at school. How was I to know that *"Mary had a little lamb, she led him in the hall, every time he raised his tail, the buckshot hit the wall"* was bad? Gil couldn't wait to tell Dad what I had done. I got blistered pretty good for that one.

Later, as Gil entered into more organized sports such as tennis, he'd line me up and whack me with his service to see how accurate he was. It got a little worse when he took up golf. I was always grateful that Gil didn't get into track and field events such as javelin throwing and shot put chunking.

Now that I am much older and I look back to those days so long ago, I wonder how Gil was able to function at all. For a little boy to be sent away to live when he is only eight or nine years old has to have some effect on a little fellow. Gil had every right to be extremely frustrated, those frustrations I'm sure he took out on me 'cause I got to stay at home on weekends.

As time went by, I wondered why Dad and Alice treated Gil

like they did. I never learned the answer. I used to tell folks these stories and we'd all feel sorry for Gil til one day someone asked me where I'd lived from the time I was eight til I was sixteen.

About the time I was eight, Dad and Alice figured it would be good for me if I didn't have to catch the bus so early in the morning and they moved me into Buda to live. We lived way back in the ranch and it was a chore to make it to the school bus on dark winter mornings. It got even worse when it rained, 'cause all our ranch roads were just dirt. So perhaps there was some good reason to send me into town during the week. At least I got to come home on the weekends. Gil never did.

Living in a complete fantasy world helped. I was always daydreaming that if I stood on one foot at exactly the right place after they dropped me off on Sunday evenings, that surely they would look back and see me with the tears streaming down my face and come back and tell me that they had changed their minds and I could start living at the ranch again. It never happened.

The first family I lived with was the Armbrusters. They lived for a time just over the railroad tracks in Buda. Later they moved out across from the Giberson Dairy, but then they moved back into Buda.

Living next to the tracks is interesting. The first night I spent there, the trains ran all night, and they were so close to the house that it shook like a leaf. I figured I'd never get a good night's sleep again. That's the only memory I have on the subject, 'cause after a night or two, I would have fallen asleep even if the trains had been running *through* the house.

The Armbrusters were poor hard working folk and I'm sure they needed the meager amount my folks were paying them to keep me, it being the depression and all. Mrs. Armbruster was a very frugal woman and she had a house full of boys, all hers, along with me. I think she had a baby boy right after I got there. Anyway, I remember that when we chewed any gum, when we

87

finished with it, she would stick it to the kitchen wall just above the wood stove and when we got home in the evening after school and wanted another run at it, she'd go peel one off the wall and give to us. I'm not sure til this day whether she marked them or not or whether it was first-come first-serve in the afternoon.

Another thing she did was serve us fried white bread in a skillet for breakfast—every single morning. I think she fried it in either some sort of oil or maybe in butter, if we had any, and then poured Karo syrup over it. It was what she called poor folk's pancakes. I kinda got where I liked it. It's a wonder all my teeth didn't rot and fall out.

Later Dad and Alice moved me in with the Montagues who owned or ran the old cafe in Buda. It was located just a couple of doors down from where the old bank building still stands. Buda has the reputation of having the only bank in the country that was robbed in the 1930s by a woman bandit. It never opened after that.

Mr. and Mrs. Montague were the salt of the earth. I don't recall what he did, maybe run the cafe while she did the cooking. She was always very kind to me. I don't know how long I stayed there, a year or two, but that time contains nothing but good memories. I do remember that I was there in 1945, 'cause that's when the war in Europe ended and Mrs. Montague's boy, Bill, came home from the war. I remember Mrs. Montague getting me up one morning to get me ready for school, and as she did, she told me in very stern terms not to go into the back room 'cause her son was home from the war, where he'd been fighting for four years, and if I startled him and woke him, he'd holler and hit me. You may rest assured it was several days before I ventured to the rear bedroom of the cafe, even though we all lived in the back.

In 1945 things went to hell in a hand basket. Dad and Alice figured I needed to be moved to the military academy in San Marcos. I have never figured out why. It was horrible, just like being in jail. For the first time, I couldn't go home on weekends. I could only go on occasions when I could get a pass. That period of my life was completely miserable. I had to stay there for fifteen months, until the spring of 1946. Gil moved out of Mona's house in that year to go to the big university, so Dad and Alice moved me in with Mona in Austin and things got a little better. It was not until the summer of 1947 that I was allowed to move back home again. Then to make things worse, Dad sold the north part of the ranch to the Rutherfords. It was the old home place where I had been raised.

Even though I'd been able to go home for many of the weekends and the summers during those years, I still remember that I was only eight years old when they started farming me out, and I was sixteen before I got to move back full time. That's pretty pitiful.

The Ultimate in Fly Fishing

*O*ur part of the ranch had miles of Onion Creek running through it. May's Water Hole itself was nearly a mile long and was probably ten to fifteen feet deep. The only time it's been low or dry in my lifetime was in 1957 at the end of our terrible '50s drought. My father had never known it dry since they bought the country in 1902. I have never been a fisherman, but my father was an ardent one.

Onion Creek is a prime game fish creek. I didn't know what that meant until one time I asked Dad why everyone wanted to come out and fish. That was before Texas started building tanks and lakes all over the ranches, all stocked with fish. The '50's drought taught us that. Dad said it was because the creek had no rough fish in it.

There is a set of falls in the creek down toward Buda, and when the creek gets up on a rise and rushes toward the Colorado River, fish of all kinds immediately start upstream—Mother Nature's way of restocking the hinterlands. Gar and suckers, bass and perch, crappie, catfish, etc., all start for the back country, but when they hit the falls at Buda, for some reason only the game fish can swim it. The rough gar and suckers can't swim over the falls, hence, the upper creek has always been prime game fishing habitat.

When Dad came home from one of his long jaunts on the polo circuit, the first thing he wanted to do was head for the creek and go fishing. He loved it. I can still remember him driving in one day from Shreveport with a big load of horses, the old black stud Smooth Sailing among them. As soon as he unloaded all the horses and had all of them in their stalls but Smooth, he'd rush in the house, change clothes, grab his bamboo fly rod, and "fly" filled hat, and head back to the barn.

The reason he headed back toward the barn was 'cause Dad had two ways of fly fishing. One was the traditional way of wading out until nothing but your eyeballs and arms were showing in the water, and the other was fishing off of old Smooth. Smooth loved it, and Dad knew he wanted to go, kinda like me and Inky. So back to the barn he went, throwing the English saddles in the tack room. He'd fetch out his old ropin' saddle, pitch it on Smooth, stick his .30-30 in the rifle scabbard, and climb on board.

Now Smooth had been in that antique trailer probably for twenty-four hours and was a tad stiff, but for a big thoroughbred, around 17 hands, he had a fine cowhorse lope. So Dad would tie his four stringers, two to each side of the saddle horn, and with "I'll see you later this evenin'," hit a long lope for May's Water Hole.

Either he was back in thirty minutes with a scowl and "Fish weren't biting," or it'd be a little after dark and the stringers would be absolutely filled, nearly hanging to the ground with fish. He'd turn on one of the Coleman lanterns and in just a few minutes they'd all be cleaned and Dad would head for the kitchen. Alice had the old wood stove up and roaring and Dad would get out the iron skillet. After rolling a bunch of those fish in cornmeal, he'd drop them in that hot skillet full of oil. My mouth starts watering when I remember that wonderful smell to this day.

But, I got ahead of my story. 'Cause you see, when Dad got to the creek, instead of getting off old Smooth like anybody else

would and tie him to a tree, Dad rode him right out in the deep water til the water was up so high that Smooth nearly had to swim, and Dad turned him up or down stream and old Smooth would start walking real slow and Dad would commence to work that bamboo rod like a violin.

He'd whip that rod back and forth, sometimes running the thread through his teeth til he could hit a spot way over toward the other bank just down below a big rock that stuck out. He'd whack into a three or four pound bass and you could hear him holler all the way to the house. Old Smooth would ease along, letting that cool water sooth his aching bones and both of them had a ball.

I'm sorry I never got a picture of the two of them except the one that is etched in my memory.

I recently found a picture of my father on Smooth, stock saddle, .30-30 and all. It hangs in a special place.

Horse Training

I eased out of bed one weekend morning, and after making a shashay through the kitchen to see what I could munch on, I worked my way out into the side yard to see what the early morning might hold. It was fall and there was a little nip in the air so I was about to head back inside to get my jacket when I happened to glance over toward the horse barn and noticed a great big hole in the side in it that I know had not been there the evening before.

Turns out Dad had been "stickin' and ballin'" (training) a bunch of ponies down on the polo field for several days in preparation for one of his long trips during polo season. He always bought lots of horses out of the Junction, Texas, country 'cause it was rough country, real rocky, and horses that are raised in real rocky country will never fall down with you. Dad wouldn't keep a horse on the ranch that would fall with a fellow.

Dad was a first class horse trainer, but he was rough. If a horse didn't do what he wanted him to do, it was Katy-bar the bedroom door as far as Dad was concerned. He'd spur and quirt him til he did what Dad wanted. That's why High Water was such a fine ol' horse—he'd been through Dad's school of hard knocks and he knew he'd better always act right or there would be heck to pay.

Well, it turns out one of the new ponies Dad had recently acquired from Roy Stubbs, Dad's main horse trader out of

Johnson City, was a little cold jawed. I really didn't know what it meant til I was explained the whole thing. Seems that when Dad was working this one particular pony the day before, he couldn't get him to stop on the dime and give back the change that Dad required. So after "chousing" the pony pretty good, the pony probably just came completely unglued, and then he went completely "coldjawed" on Dad. That's when the heat of the moment took over.

By that time Dad had whipped the pony all the way up toward the house to teach him a few manners, but when the pony still wouldn't stop at all, Dad figured he'd teach him the ultimate lesson. He loped him about 150 yards from the barn, whirled him around, and with a yell that would have been good coming from a Comanche, started for the side of the barn, whipping and spurring him at every jump, knowing when they got to the side of the big two-story barn that the pony would stop.

Dad told me later that by the time they hit the side of the barn, he was probably doing about 110 and the good little ol' pony never broke stride. Well, you've seen cartoons where when something ran through a wall, it left the hole in the exact shape of what went through it. I swear that's what it almost looked like. The shape of a horse and rider, the rider with a hat on and his spurs jingling out to one side. Well, not quite, but that's what I imagined.

Turns out the poor little pony would have run plumb through the whole barn if his head hadn't hit a big ceiling joist and knocked him as cold as a bucket of cucumbers. Dad had gone flying off to crash elsewhere and as will happen to folks who are wild and crazy, didn't hurt him one bit. He crawled out of the barn and went and got a bucket of water out of the horse trough and threw it on the little pony and then went to the house to phone Roy to come get the poor little devil.

So much for one day's horse training.

The Dude and the Wild Hog

Back in the 1930s and the early 1940s, there were a lot of wild hogs on the ranch, not javelinas, but wild hogs weighing 400 pounds or better. Today they are called feral. Since the ranch was so big and had so much creek country, it was fabulous habitat for just about anything wild and woolly, including my father. So when he came home from one of his long polo trips, he liked to unwind by doing lots of hunting and fishing.

A lot of times he would bring someone home with him and one particular time he brought Gardner (Gardy) Abbott. Gardy was from Cleveland, Ohio, from one of the old families up there. The thought of coming to Texas always fascinated him, 'cause to come down and play cowboy on a big Texas ranch with a real Texas cowboy was quite a treat.

Dad kept an arsenal of guns around, which were always loaded. Nothing he hated worse than an unloaded gun. He figured when you needed one, you needed it in a hurry and it was idiotic to scurry around looking for the bullets. He also believed in strict gun etiquette that he taught me. It has fared me well these many years. He was right of course, and growing up in that environment I was made to understand that principle and I believe it to this day.

His favorite rifle in those days was a Winchester .30-30 model 64. It was a special order rifle that had a longer than standard barrel. He carried it everywhere he went, horseback especially. I have it to this day.

He'd not been home more than a day or so when he jumped a big bunch of wild hogs up in a pasture we called the "1200." So the following morning he saddled up old Smooth for himself and another pony for Gardy and off they went on a wild hog hunt.

The south boundary of that pasture was Onion Creek which was prime country for hogs. Dad cut northwest from the ranchhouse for about five or six miles until he got up into the middle of that area. What he was looking for was a good fat sow to kill 'cause they are prime eating. There was no reason to kill a boar, 'cause they stunk to high heaven, and you never ate them unless they were very young.

They hadn't gone over a mile through that pasture when Dad spotted the bunch he was looking for. There was an area down in the flats below where he and Gardy were holed up that was real boggy. The hogs always hung out in that area when they weren't disturbed.

He eased off of ol' Smooth and motioned for Gardy to do the same and then both of them commenced to slip off down where Dad could get a shot at the one he wanted. Gardy was not armed, just Dad. They hadn't gone over a couple of hundred yards toward the bunch when all of a sudden they came upon a big ol' sow that had been lying up nearby unseen.

She gave a big snort and took off not fifty yards from where the two of them were huddled. Just as she hit a little opening, Dad cut loose at her and gut-shot her by mistake. Well, with that she tore up the side of the hill running over everything in sight and all the other hogs scattered like a covey of quail.

The one thing you *don't* want to do is wound a big wild hog. Their tusks are about two to five inches long, depending on whether they are male or female, with the females having ones slightly shorter. This old mama had a pair about three inches long that would let her cut through a trace chain if she could get a whack at it.

All of a sudden everything got very quiet and they couldn't hear which way the ol' sow was running. Dad told Gardy to follow him real close, 'cause the sow had holed up. He started working his way up a cowpath where he found a good blood trail. He told Gardy to get prepared 'cause that sow would most likely charge them when she saw them. He instructed Gardy to get up in a tree when that happened and everything would be all right.

They hadn't gone but a 100 yards when Dad heard a thumping and ripping sound in conjunction with a lot of grunting and all sorts of carrying on. He eased up the trail a few more yards and spotted the sow sitting down beside a big Spanish oak. The sow was whacking the tree with her tusks and knocking off a big slab of bark with every swing of her head. About that time, she spotted Dad, and was up and at him in a flash.

That sow was covering the ground like a race horse when Dad jumped up in a little low hanging cedar tree that had a fork in it and shot the hog right between the eyes, putting an end to her misery.

He then hopped down and looked around for Gardy, who had been two feet behind him when the fight started, but he was now nowhere to be seen. So Dad started back down the trail aways and gave a big "hallo." Dad said that he received an answer about a half a mile away and to his amazement it was, of course, Gardy. It seems that when the sow broke for Dad, Gardy broke for home. And while she only covered about 30 yards, Gardy must have covered 300.

Gardy was headed for the house. He figured that latching on the front end of one of those ol' wild hogs was not his cup of tea. Dad laughed about that tale for 50 years.

Never Unhorsed!

I was tape recording Dad one time and started asking him questions about the polo days and such, just wondering what his reactions might be. I asked him how he prepared for a game and did he ever worry about how good or tough an opposing team might be.

He started telling me that polo was never a sport for him. It was hard work—lots of hours training horses, and then the games on Sunday afternoon. Dad had a big ranch, but he was never a man of money wealth, his wealth lay in other areas. He had to be his own boss; he never would work for anyone. Many's the time he'd tell Alice that so and so who owned some big company in Cleveland or Boston wanted him to ride on his team but he would never do it.

He paid his own way for eight years on the polo circuit by buying horses out of the Junction-Rocksprings country of Texas, training the heck out of them, and then selling them to his wealthy friends up east. People were standing in line for his horses. Dad was mighty rough on a horse, and if that pony survived the Wild Bill training period, you could bet your bottom dollar the horse either was the best on the field that day or was equal to the best.

I think Dad was kinda proud that he played rough, just like

101

he was when he played football. He played lots of football at South West Normal in San Marcos before anyone had any pads to speak of, so when he said he played polo rough, I figured he meant *rough*.

Anyway, turns out there was some polo team that had been whipping on everybody pretty good and Dad and his bunch were scheduled to play them the following Sunday in a tournament. One of that bunch had obviously been loud talking about what he was going to do to the Texans, so Dad told his teammates, "Just leave him to me."

Now when a polo game starts, there are four folks on either side, and when the umpire pitches the polo ball into the mass of eight ponies, the name of the game was to hit the ball out of that mess and work it down field until one of them drove it between the goal posts and scored. A full game is eight chukkas, but often in club matches, four or six chukkas are played that last about seven minutes each, so you had to have a fine string of ponies 'cause you wear them down pretty quick. Normally horses are changed after each chukka.

Dad usually kept ol' Smooth for the latter part of the game, but on this day he said he saddled him up first. Even when you have many good horses over the years, there comes that time when you have a really outstanding one, and old Smooth was *that* one for my father. He and Dad were absolutely one solid entity on the field together. Smooth was the only stud horse Dad ever played on. Usually studs are too ornery and too hard to manage, but Smooth pretty well kept his stud disposition in tow, and he would do anything Dad asked him to do—*anything!*

So Dad saddled him up and eased out on the playing field and got lined up on his side of the field, which was with his back to his own goal. Dad wore number "4," 'cause he was a back, or the goalie. It was his job to keep the opposing team from scoring. So if the opposing team picked up the ball when it was thrown in by the umpire, it was Dad's job to fall back and guard the goal.

Well, everybody got ready, all prancing around and such, and the umpire pitched the bamboo-root ball into the eight horses' legs, and instead on whirling ol' Smooth back down the field to play goalie, Dad whirled him at the guy who'd been badmouthing them. With two big jumps, he jumped ol' Smooth right in the big middle of that fellow and his horse and went right over the top of them, rolling them over like pumpkins. Ol' Smooth never broke stride!

Dad started laughing as he told the story, 'cause he said for the whole balance of the game, all he had to do was act like he was going to make a run at the fellow, and he'd squall like a kid and run plumb off the field. As Dad put it, "I broke him of sucking eggs!"

I then asked him if *he'd* ever been unhorsed in a game, and he got rather red-faced and angry, and retorted, *never!*, but then he relaxed a bit and grinned, and said, "but I unhorsed someone else in just about every game I played in!"

Sad Days

*D*ad was real hard on horses. He wouldn't keep one on the ranch thirty minutes if the horse fell with him. If Roy Stubbs brought one down that stumbled or fell with him, Dad'd get on the crank phone and holler at Roy to get down to the ranch from Johnson City and get that blankity-blank pony off his ranch. He just had a real phobia about it. I suspect, if you have lived your whole life aboard a horse, there were just certain rules you had to abide by. This was one that Dad had.

It must have been around 1943, 'cause Dad quit polo in 1939 and retired ol' Smooth. We were working a bunch of cattle just north of the house and our neighbor to the north, Oldham Rogers, was there helping out. For some reason Dad had put him on ol' Smooth and his son, Joe Bob, on my horse, High Water. He had saddled another pony for me to ride.

We had just bunched up this little dab of cattle when a cow broke out and Oldham loped out to head her off. All of a sudden ol' Smooth stumbled and went head over tea-kettle. Well, I thought Oldham was dead. He was skinned from head to toe. Ol' Smooth had just stumbled over a bunch of loose rocks and Oldham fell right in amongst them. I remember Joe Bob going by me like a shot, spurring High Water at every jump. I had never seen High Water run, 'cause with me he didn't, but he was flying!

The house wasn't but about a mile and in no time Alice was back with Joe Bob and the car. By that time Dad had Oldham up on his feet and they loaded him into the car so Alice could take him into Buda to Dr. Lauderdale's. It turned out he was all right, just pretty bunged up, but it didn't turn out so well for Ol' Smooth.

Dad led him up to the house and tied him up and went in and phoned down to the dairy which is now Giberson's. I'm not sure if they owned it then or not. Anyway, he asked those folks if they needed a good stud horse. They said they did, so Dad loaded up his old faithful friend in the trailer that afternoon and hauled him down to near Buda and never mentioned his name again until late in life when I asked about him.

I always felt so bad about that. It seemed to me that Smooth should have been able to spend his last days on our beautiful ranch, but to Dad a rule was a rule, and that was that!

105

Part V

SMA, FOOTBALL

San Marcos Baptist Academy

After several years of having to pick me up on weekends, Alice and Dad got tired of the hassle of dealing with their only son still at home and decided it was in my best interest to ship me off to a boarding school. The closest one was good old SMA. I can't think of anything worse in this world than having to go or ever having gone to San Marcos Baptist Academy. I was about 12 years old and it was the pits.

When you are placed into a conservative Baptist school where you are told that just about anything you did was some sorta "sin," you suddenly began to feel a great deal of anxiety over your future welfare. I figured that I was close to being a goner.

Of course, all of those 12-year-old reactions were beyond my understanding at the time. I certainly wasn't going to talk or tell anyone about what I was doing. The only one that ever listened to me was Inky, and he figured he didn't look good in a SMA uniform. So I got the notion that my little bitty sittin'-down-place was being hung out to dry. Little did I know, redemption was near at hand—Baptist style!

One thing you had to do at SMA was go to the Baptist church a lot. Sunday morning for worship service, Sunday night for fellowship, and Wednesday night for choir practice, and Oh, praise the Lord, if we could have just had a few more revivals. That meant you got to go *every* night. This being a military school and all, they'd march your little heinie down there whether you figured you needed it or not.

I had never been to church that regular and everybody kept asking me if I'd been saved. Saved from what? From whom? I asked my mother and she being one who believed one had to be a mature adult to understand such fundamental things, never did tell me anything. She was just glad I was down there where I was not under foot at the ranch all the time and don't worry about whether you're saved or not. Well, brother, I'm here to tell you that won't cut it with those Baptists. They are serious folks when it comes to the "saving part."

They made us sit pretty close up toward the front of the church so when the preacher went to ranting and raving and leaning way out over the congregation, he was basically looking right down on top of us and waving his mighty finger and squalling at the top of his lungs that if you didn't find God and get saved *right then*, when you walked out of the church, a big gravel truck or maybe a bolt of lightning was either going to hit you or mash you flat where your own mother wouldn't recognize you and if you hadn't been "saved" the big ol' Devil was going to come get you and take you off to Hell! All in one breath! Being the country boy I was, I sure didn't want to go to Hell, and besides that, the preacher had me scared spitless. Where was old Inky and my mother when I really needed them?

By the time I'd made about my twelfth revival, I knew hell and damnation were my only future unless I could get myself "saved." So on the next Sunday when the preacher started inviting all us sinners down to the front to the tune of "Just As I Am" or something like that, I bailed out of my pew and went scooting down to tell the preacher I'd do anything to keep from going to Hell, or words close to that.

Oh, you would have thought he'd found his first real sinner in the whole world when I hit the front. He wanted to know if I'd found Jesus! Well, I allowed as how Jesus and I weren't really on a first name basis at that time but I figured I'd better answer in the affirmative, 'cause I was sure afraid that if I left that church that day *unsaved*, the preacherman would whistle up that gravel truck and my spindly little behind was gonna be flat as fourteen pancakes.

Well, I left that day feeling a lot like a big honeycomb rock had been lifted off of my head. Little did I know that the saving part had just begun. The real fun was to be the following Sunday when I got to be—you guessed it—*baptized*. You can't be saved unless you "be" baptized, which for the Baptists is the most fun part. That's why they have those really big horse troughs up in the front of the church covered with that dark curtain. On certain Sundays, they jerked the curtain open with a loud, *voila!* BEHOLD, and then some poor lost soul will be drug into the horse trough. But I'm getting ahead of myself.

I wrote and told mother that I was "partially" saved and the "good part" was going to take place the following Sunday if they wanted to attend. She declined, feeling probably it would be slightly beneath her elevated dignity to witness her 12-year-old son making such an irrational, emotional decision that should be left only to consenting adults, *whatever that meant*.

Well, come next Sunday, with the party about to commence, I scrubbed myself plumb raw and put on my best 12-year-old clothes and went forth to be baptized in the name of the Lord. I was in for a surprise! Part of the fun of being a Baptist minister is baptizing folks. The preacher went on and on about the devil, cement trucks, and lightning. Finally came the time to baptize the newly confessed sinners.

I was the first one. They make you go up and get behind the pulpit where there is a little door to the horse trough. It's kinda like the squeeze pen next to the dipping vats where Dad used to force the cows. When you opened the little gate, they'd all jump in the vat and get all their ticks killed.

Well, there I was and all of a sudden, the preacher flung open the little bitty door, and motioned for me to join him in the horse trough. He had come in from the other side and was already in there with water up to his waist. Now remember, I was only 12 years old and real little for my age. I started stepping off those stairs into that water with my shoes off but with my pants and my white shirt and some sorta bed sheet they had flung on me and man was that water cold!

By the time I reached the bottom of the tank, the water was up to my armpits. The preacher was all revved up by the time I got to him, and with a shout of glee he grabbed me by the scruff of the neck and commenced to dunk me in that horse trough, jerking me out every now and then, while admonishing the devil and anything else to "*be gone*"!

I tried to grab a gulp of air in between dunkings, but the more he dunked me, the more fervent he became, and finally I held up one of my hands that I surrendered and that if he'd ever let me out of that damn horse trough I'd believe *anything* he wanted me to believe.

Thank God for one thing. The Baptists swear that one good baptizing is all you need and I'm here to tell you they are telling you the truth! If I ever get reincarnated, I'm going to come back as a Methodist or an Episcopalian, 'cause they only sprinkle you. I'd lot rather that happen the second time around than someone doing his level best to flat out drown you!

Inky stayed in his heathen ways. He was smarter than I was. He knew when good folks were good folks and you didn't need all that extemporaneous mess. He knew how folks were supposed to treat one another. It took me half a life time to realize his teachings were the best. He was always more mature than me. Inky figured that kids will be kids and there was no sin in that. He also figured when you became an adult you should try to act like one.

Six Man Football

Mother finally took pity on me and my crying and gnashing of teeth over having to go to SMA, so when brother Gil moved out of Grandmother Mona's house on 1215 Parkway in Austin to go to the University of Texas, I moved in. That was in 1946. I stayed there until after the north part of the ranch was sold to Pat Rutherford in 1947. Then, when our new house was built on the south side of the ranch in 1948, I moved back home for the first time in years and entered dear ol' Kyle High School.

*T*here weren't that many folks living in the hinterlands of Central Texas in 1948 just after the Great War. So after Dad sold the north part of the Kuykendall Ranch, we got our house built just in time for me to start school at dear ol' Kyle High in the fall of 1949.

I had played intermural sports when I had gone to some of the Austin schools while I was in transition, but being very little, there was no way I could go out for, or be received on, any regular team of any kind, that is until I showed up at Kyle. Kyle was kinda like the military—all you had to have was blood in your body and you were needed 'cause there weren't but about thirty to forty kids in the whole high school as opposed to the hundreds or perhaps a thousand kids at Austin High when I was there.

I was fresh meat. I remember Ann Miller towered over me

my junior year. I probably stood 5'3" and weighed a whopping 125 pounds. Coach Black looked at me as one of his new prime substitutes for his football team—*six* man football, that is. He had six starters but few substitutes. I don't remember how many extras we had, but I don't recall that we had over twelve or thirteen total who went out for football that fall and a bunch of them were smaller than I was. We were a powerhouse.

Six man football is wild and woolly and high scoring. Most of the games ended with scores such as 75 to 50. There are three on the line and three in the backfield and there had to be a clear pass in the backfield as a handoff. You couldn't just hand the ball to your backs. You had to pitch it to them or it was a foul, or the quarterback could pass it to them. I think David Allen was quarterback both my years of 1948 and 1949. He could be quarterback 'cause he was already grown. Some of the rest of us had to wait a while.

I don't remember all of our schedule in those years, but I know we played Prairie Lee, Blanco, Manor, Buda, Pflugerville, and I think Dripping Springs. And of course, Buda was our big rival. Man, if you didn't beat Buda, you had to do 400 laps around the football field *after* the game. Well, not quite 400, but close. And you better not show your face around the Bon Ton grocery store for several days or Mr. Word or Mr. Bales would have a little talk with you, not to mention Mrs. Wallace at school.

We played Buda several games into our season and my little tiny butt had been keeping the bench pretty warm. We played Buda in Kyle in 1948 with a really big crowd. I think even my Dad showed up to see if his runt kid would get to play and hold up the family honor.

Football fields were different in those days. Somebody just scraped off a level place behind the schoolhouse, ran some lines across it, pitched off most of the rocks before game time and called it "ready to play." I distinctly remember the Kyle alums would gather just before game time every Friday night and try to throw most of the bigger rocks off the field that had turned up since the previous Friday night. The scars on my elbows and knees didn't entirely heal til after I was forty years old.

I'm pretty sure David Allen was quarterback and probably Edward Schmeltekopf was one of the backs that year. What I really remember was that Buda had been beating the tar out of everyone 'cause they had a running back who had come back to school on a World War I scholarship. Every time he got the ball, he ran for a touchdown. For some reason I think his name was Lawrence something and he lived out on the Giberson place west of Buda.

We had a fellow on our team who was tough as nails, though. If it hadn't been for a small happening, I'd probably never have seen the glory of playing for the great Kyle Panthers. Sometime after the game started, the WWI fellow got the ball and was headed for a certain score when he was blasted by Jack Peoples, one of our main defensive players, who was scared of neither man nor beast and would have tackled a bulldozer had one been coming down the field.

As fate would have it, Jack got his man, but in the process he broke his leg plumb off. I mean he was going south and it was going north. Everybody got out of the stands and drug poor ol' Jack off the field so he wouldn't be in the way. Right in the middle of everything Coach Black hollered at me, "Get your little runty butt in there. What do you think you been practicing for all year?" Or words to that effect. I was petrified. But duty called and that was that.

I was so little that none of the uniforms fit me. I looked like an orphan who had just been plucked from the brush. My number 19 shirt was so big it hung down to my knees when it wasn't tucked in. My pants were so floppy that they hung down below toward my ankles and when I hit the ground, which was often, my poor knees hit first, the knee-pads never being in the right place when I needed them most, hence there was no skin on them at all. You could turn my helmet around on my head if you didn't tighten the chin strap. If they had had duct tape in those days, Coach would have taped it on permanently.

What I remembered next has stayed with me all of these years as the first football game of my career. I obviously went in on defense. Why anyone thought I could substitute for Jack Peoples escapes me to this day. And what does Buda do but pitch the ball to ol' WWI. He came busting through the line (That's a *metaphor*. You don't bust through the line in six man football, you fly through the line.), straight at you-know-who.

He was on me like a starving dog on roadkill and I distinctly remember trying to dodge out of his way so I would not be maimed like poor ol' Jack, but he ran straight over the top of me. I mean right over. I was just traction on his way to another touchdown when his cleats got tangled up in my floppy jersey. On top of that, my helmet filled up full of rocks and dirt to the extent that he just couldn't drag me any further. After stumbling and falling for about 15 yards, dragging me as he went, he tripped and went down hard.

I'll have you know that the people in the stands came to their feet and you could have heard the Kyle fans holler all the way to Buda. "Runt" Kuykendall had saved the day!

Coach Black came running out on the field and gathered me up and hauled me off to the sidelines, all the time exulting my great feat while he poured the dirt and rocks out of my helmet and helped me put my uniform back on.

I don't remember another thing about the game. I doubt if I was allowed to play another play. Coach probably figured one "near" funeral was enough.

I will say this, though, I was allowed to play more that year and started all the games my senior year of 1949. Those are some of the most cherished memories of my life.

Some of us graduated in the spring of 1950 and some on that team graduated in the spring of 1951. Some of us went to college, some of us went to work, some of us fell on a battlefield in a far off, cold place.

I received an "invite" back in October 2001, when the "Class of 50" celebrated our 50th Anniversary at the old Kyle Gym. All of my class of 1950 with the exception of Edward Schmeltekopf and Sue Evans showed up. We had a blast, all seven of us, plus the other classes. Kyle always throws a bunch of classes together for the reunions or there wouldn't be enough people in the old Kyle Gym to feed three hamburgers.

Six Man Football Revisited

*T*his past spring marked 50 years since I graduated from Kyle High and several things popped in my mind as I recall those days.

The fall of 1949 was the last of our football days playing for the Panthers of Kyle High School. In those days all of the classes, lower grades through the twelfth grade, were all held where the elementary school and the old Kyle Gym are today.

One particular game that comes to mind was when we played Pflugerville. I'm not sure if we played them along with Manor every year, but I think so. The football field was just to the north of the highway that runs into Pflugerville and it paralleled the highway and the hill that is there. When I say paralleled the hill, I mean the field ran at a 45 degree angle across the side of the hill so when you ran down the field, one leg was considerably shorter than the other due to the steepness of the incline. Of course, when one reversed the field, the opposite leg got the same treatment. It was kind of like running down the roof of an old hay barn, but at least you didn't fall off, maybe.

The field was pretty well grassed over which was a treat for those of us who came out of the hills where the rocks had to be thrown off the field before and after every game. I think that all of the town of Pflugerville had only one water hydrant and for some reason it was smack dab in the middle of the football field at the 50 yard line so they could water the grass every now and then. It was supposed to be either underneath the turf or at least level with it, but the old thing leaked and dripped all the time so it was a solid muddy mess out about 10-15 yards in every direction especially since a good many games had already been played on the field before we got there.

I do not remember the score, but Coach had a secret play and a secret player in the form of one James Schmeltekopf. James could throw a football a country mile. He was not normally in at quarterback, since that job went to David LaVern Allen. But on occasions Coach would put in James and have him chunk the ball several hundred yards down the field and the fastest man on the team would run down and get under it and run for the touchdown. Sounds simple, doesn't it?

Well, the job of running under James's pass fell to me since I could flat out fly. I had been clocked many times running the hundred in 22 flat so Coach sent in James and gave me the high sign to go get it! Things kinda went downhill or should I say caddy-wampus from there!

We all lined up over the ball in great anticipation. Unknown to all of us, the ball had sprung a leak. However, our brilliant center centered it anyway. James took the snap and faded back to chuck the ball to the other side of town and you-know-who took off like a bullet shot out of a gun, or maybe it was like a spit-wad.

James hauled back and let her fly. I was running as hard as my one long and one short leg would allow, looking over my shoulder to see where the ball was headed so I could get underneath it when I ran through the mudhole, stumbled over the ONLY hydrant in all Pflugerville, and fell in and under all of the mud and slosh in that part of the county.

James, in the meantime, had let fly the pass of the century, which, since the ball was nearly flat, felt like he was chunking his grandmother's Angel Food Cake. It flew about 7 and a half yards, was intercepted by one of the opposing players, who, while my team was digging me out of the mud hole, ran for a touchdown.

Those were the days!

INKY 1939-1945

Farewell, My Friend

*M*y lifelong friend who raised me died in 1946 of pneumonia. I can still see him today, curled up in the drizzling rain, not knowing any better 'cause he was an outside dog. Folks didn't let dogs in the house, at least at our ranch, in those days, and Dad was a believer that everyone and everything had to pretty well make it on their own.

Alice called me over at Mona's where I was living during the week while I went to school to give me the news. I remember I was on my way up to see Jack and Mike Roach who lived up close to Palma Plaza. I was about 14 years old at the time. I tried to tell the Roach boys what had happened and how sad I was, but they had other things on their minds.

When I got home that next weekend, Dad took me out east of the old ranch house to show me where he had buried him. It was next to a big cedar stump and I make a mental note and a promise to Inky that if it was the last thing I ever did, I'd save my money and put up a regular monument in his behalf. The sale of the ranch, teenage years, and lots of pretty girls at the Kyle High School soon separated me from that promise. Inky would have done better.

A good many years later while looking in an old trunk, I found several rolls of undeveloped film that I decided to have processed to see what was on them. To my delight, two of the rolls were of me and Inky in our heyday. The memories came tumbling back as I looked at them and my old friend.

I never did live up to my promise about getting him a regular monument and I cry when I think I failed him in that way. He would have licked all the tears from my face and admonished me to buck up, that it really didn't matter, that country dogs didn't need a monument and that "he forgave me long ago, anyway."

So ends my story of the old days about my real ol' friend and our days together growing up on a Hays County, Texas, ranch.

MARSHALL E. KUYKENDALL
Driftwood, Texas
Winter 2006